"A thrilling read and meticulously researched, *Intrepid Pursuit* calls forward a true and urgent problem facing aviation. A must read for all who fly."

Capt Reyné O'Shaughnessy, Boeing 767 Pilot, Author, Safety Expert

"Fresh and fast paced, *Intrepid Pursuit* is a captivating novel that brings to life a hidden but critical history."

William Sullivan, United Airline Airbus A320 Pilot

Intrepid Pursuit
A pilot's fight to stop a disaster decades in the making.

William Hoffman

This book is a work of fiction. Names, characters, certain organizations, people, and certain events are all products of the author's mind and are fictitious.

Copyright © 2021 by William Hoffman.

All rights reserved. Published in the United States by Amazon.

ISBN 978-1-7339068-4-5

First Edition.

To my wife

Acknowledgements

A sincere thanks to Allison Millea for her expertise guiding the development and editing of this book. Thank you also to Elin Richey for her cover design. Special thanks to friends that shared their skills in story editing, technical expertise and support to include William Sullivan, Denise and Tim Baker, Sue Dieter, Ruben Cáceres, and Brent and Trina Maki. A special thanks for Ali Selim for sharing this gift of storytelling and for his generous mentorship.

Fact

Aerotoxic Syndrome[1] is a medical emergency that has been described in passengers and crew of airliners. It is thought to be secondary to toxic exposure to an organophosphate called tricresyl phosphate (TCP), a neurotoxic component of aircraft engine oil.

---

[1]Hageman G, Pal T, Nihom J, et al. Aerotoxic Syndrome, discussion of possible diagnostic criteria. *Clinical Toxicology*. 2020; 58(5): 414-416. doi.org/10.1080/15563650.2019.1649419

"You haven't seen a tree until you've seen its shadow from the sky."

Amelia Earhart

Part 1

Chapter 1

September 2024 | Minneapolis-St. Paul International Airport
Minneapolis, Minnesota

"Minneapolis Tower, Avionica 1846, holding short runway one seven," said the co-pilot into his headset. The airliner's two IAE V2500 engines purred on the taxiway beside the 10,000-foot asphalt runway. In the crisp autumn breeze, a Delta Airlines 767 fresh from Tokyo was rolling on the taxiway while a commuter jet lined up on final approach. The co-pilot was young, with soft eyes and a plush crop of auburn hair.

"Let's run the before take-off checklist," said the captain, tightening the straps over his shoulders. He was trim with heavy lines below his eyes. He was confident and steady thanks to years at his craft. His co-pilot Cameron was eager, he'd give him that, but he had much to learn.

"Before take-off checklist," said the co-pilot. He was smiling but focused. New to the airline, he was proud of his seven months with the budget carrier. He was prepared and hopeful of making a good impression with the senior aviator. Like a tango, the junior first officer and captain began:

```
"Elevator."
```

William Hoffman

SET FOR TAKE-OFF

"Flaps."

ONE

"Spoilers."

RETRACTED

As Cameron listed each item on the checklist, the captain double checked the controls. Outside, an airliner lifted into the air and the Minneapolis-St Paul International Airport bustled beyond. The terminal was sprawling to their right and the historic grounds of Fort Snelling was settled to their left. Trees, heavy with dark foliage, bordered the field.

Departing on the final leg of their trip, Captain Frank Brewer and First Officer Cameron Fischer were returning home after four busy days of bussing vacationers to and from their base in Tampa. The entire airline was working overtime. In the days leading up to another school year, airplanes were full, and revenue was high. There was little interest in much else beyond keeping the planes moving. Avionica Airlines was a relatively new low-cost carrier with fewer than ten years in operation, but it was seizing bigger portions of the market by the month. Despite the long hours and cheap motels, Cameron was hardworking and loved his job. He was 24 years old and lived for this lifestyle. Both of his parents were airline pilots and he had always wanted to follow in their footsteps. He was loyal to the company who had given him his first job, no matter how precarious it was. Cameron couldn't deny the airplanes were old, even by budget airline standards, but it didn't bother him.

Through radio chatter, the controller finally cleared the battered A320 for departure. Frank pushed the throttles forward and the engines bellied the airliner forward to the center line. At the head of the runway, the 155-seat commuter came to a stop. The asphalt strip faced south, towards the oak and spruce forest thriving along the valley of the Minnesota River. The morning sky was clearing after a brief shower and songbirds were marking the beginning of a new day.

Intrepid Pursuit

Eyeing the controls one final time, the captain positioned his left hand on the control stick and his right on the throttles. "You ready, Cameron?" He adjusted the mic on his headset.

Cameron tucked the checklist away and settled into his seat. He was happy to be finally underway after all the issues they had endured over the past 24 hours.

"All set, boss," he said. They had been scheduled to return to Tampa yesterday morning, but there had been some hiccups. A mechanical problem had brought them back to the gate and delayed them by an entire day. A hydraulic leak in one of the circuits hadn't been an easy fix and it had taken the entire afternoon to find a mechanic. But finally, it all seemed settled. Navigating these sorts of things was all new to Cameron, but he trusted the captain. When he said it was time to go, he didn't ask questions. In truth, he was exhausted and was ready to get home anyway.

With the throttles forward, the engines began to spool. The captain released the brakes, and the airliner began to accelerate down the center line. The aircraft pressed lighter on the concrete as their speed grew. Frank's eyes were forward while Cameron's were on the instruments. Over each crack in the asphalt, the aircraft shuddered.

"Eighty knots," called the first officer.

"Roger, eighty knots," responded the captain, his focus still ahead. The nose wheeled perfectly down the center line as their momentum grew.

The dance continued until enough lift brought them into the sky.

"Positive rate," called the first officer, seeing their altitude building. The 33-year-old aircraft climbed higher.

"Roger," Frank said with an even tempo. "Gear up."

The first officer pulled the airliner's landing gear below the wings. The engines transitioned from a bursting roar to a metallic ring. Beneath the nose, the airplane was climbing over the Mall of America. The sprawling building had a 100-acre footprint, complete with an indoor amusement park housing three roller coasters. Two massive parking ramps made it easy to spot from the air. Cameron caught a glance of it disappearing behind them, thinking to himself how beautiful the world was from this vantage point.

Controllers instructed the crew to turn southeast and climb. The captain pulled the throttles back and the first officer retracted the flaps. Now passing through 3,000 feet, the Airbus banked left over the winding path of the Minnesota River. Frank admired the lush summertime greens beginning to change in the grassy marshes below. Behind them, the peaks of the Minneapolis skyline, only a few miles from St. Paul, grew from the earth. With the wings level again, they headed south and towards home.

"Avionica 1864, climb and maintain one two thousand feet and maintain current heading," the controller called out a final time. "Contact Minneapolis Departure on 124.7."

It felt routine. Their cadence was drumming with syncopation, consistent and predictable. Like the thousands of hours Captain Frank Brewer had flown, each moment complied with the strict rules of flight.

Until something changed.

Where there should have been action, there was silence. An unusual pause interrupted the beat of the departure cockpit. The co-pilot said nothing. The lull, unsettling and full, weighed in the air as each second passed. Finally, the captain looked to the first officer.

"Cameron," the captain shot curtly. The controller's radio call was left unanswered. "That's us."

Still the first officer remained silent. Cameron was looking out through the right window and Frank couldn't see his face. The boy remained perfectly still. "Cameron!" Frank's voice was a little louder now, with a new uneasiness in his tone. Still, there was no response.

Confused, the captain finally spoke into the foam microphone just below his bottom lip. He confirmed the controller's direction and adjusted the autopilot, his words lingering no longer than required. Now flying over the southern Twin Cities, a new uneasiness was growing.

"Cameron, are you…" the captain started, but he couldn't finish. What interrupted him came so suddenly that Frank could only watch. Instead of responding to the controller, the young co-pilot began to cough. Like a switch being flipped, it was acute and violent. The hacking was staccato, and so rapid that the young man had to gasp for air. Frank watched in disbelief.

"What's going on?" Frank called over the croup. Cameron didn't answer. In fact, things were quickly worsening. The color in his face became dusky and grey, and his eager eyes faded. He leaned forward, expelling hot saliva into his fist. "Cameron!" The captain barked as though he was trying to snap him out of a trance. The first officer only slumped further forward into his shoulder straps.

Then, the captain smelled it.

The odor was sharp and chemical; it cut into his nostrils like a knife. "Jesus," he said to himself. He felt a tightness around his own windpipe now. They were just passing through 5,000 feet, some 20 miles from the runway. He brought his hand up and also began to cough. Unfortunately, it was only getting worse. The scent expanded, becoming more powerful with every second. Around his lungs, it seemed to be tightening its grip. Then he noticed a vague fog beginning to accumulate in the cockpit. It was subtle, and Frank would not have caught it if it weren't for his eyes and throat that were now beginning to burn.

"What is this?" Frank said to himself. He could hear the wariness in his own voice. He looked back to his co-pilot, whose body was limp and collapsed forward. The boy looked sick, that was for certain, but Frank was hardly certain of anything else. Something was wrong and they were only getting further away from the help they needed.

"Frank..." the co-pilot cried out. It was the first thing the boy had said since they departed. His voice was weak and wounded.

"Tell me what's happening, Cameron!" the captain demanded. His training was taking over, and he was studying the controls. When he looked back to the co-pilot, he realized things were worse than he had imagined.

The co-pilot's face was growing red, and his eyes were wide. The muscles along his spine were contracting so he arched back, stiff as a board. His arms were tight to his chest and his shoulder straps fought against his force. When his head was pulled completely back, Cameron let out a deafening cry from the back of his throat.

"Goddamn it!" said Frank fighting the urge to cough in the growing haze.

As the airliner climbed through 6,500 feet, Cameron began to seize. His arms flexed and extended chaotically while his legs began to jerk. His eyes were being pulled up into his head so only the whites could be seen. It was unlikely anything Frank had seen before. The captain mumbled something to himself and pulled his eyes away. His training was urging him to act, and he needed to focus. If they were going to get through whatever was happening, he needed to do something.

Beside his left knee, a grey box housed an oxygen mask. He popped the top open and pulled it over his face. When the mask was snug, a burst of fresh oxygen pumped into his lungs. It was sweet relief, like a rope cut free from around his neck. As he took a second breath, he thought about how he had known this day could come.

With his co-pilot seizing and smoke filling his aircraft, Captain Frank Brewer had to make a split-second decision. His eyes were burning and his skull was throbbing. He reached over his head, deploying the oxygen masks in the passenger cabin. Their situation was dire and seemed to be growing grimmer with each second. Frank flipped off the autopilot and held the control sidestick in hand. He had gotten them into this situation, and he alone would have to get them out of it.

Intrepid Pursuit

"Minneapolis Departure, Avionica 1864," said the captain evenly into the mic. His heart was throbbing in his chest as his mind raced. He considered their options, knowing they were few. There was only a few minutes worth of oxygen in the tanks. The smoke grew and Cameron's seizure continued. Frank dipped the wings to the left and pulled back, knowing they had to get back to the field. "We're declaring an emergency," said the captain into the radio. "We need to land immediately."

He could only pray there was enough oxygen in the tanks.

As Captain Brewer piloted his ailing plane back to earth, he was plagued by all the warning signs. He thought about the maintenance problems the day before, knowing he should've listened to his gut. He knew this could've happened; in fact he had known it for years. He had turned a blind eye to it, thinking it could never happen to him. But now here he was, with hundreds of lives in his hands, and grim reality closing in. It wasn't the first time that this chemical had filled an airplane full of people, and it was only a matter of time until it happened again.

Chapter 2

September 2024| University of North Dakota
Grand Forks, North Dakota

"On the sandy beaches of North Carolina, the sun was just rising across the brisk morning horizon." Professor Julie Sampers spoke with vigor and grace. "Two men, brothers in fact, from a quiet town in Ohio, stood beside their contraption in the windy planes of Kitty Hawk. Together, they were ready to make history."

The lecture hall was full, with tapered amphitheater seats that bowed from back to front. A whiteboard, polished after the summer's recess, was hanging at the front. Three towering windows permitted light into the lecture hall while maps and figures papered the walls. The 138 students, all freshmen who were ripe with anticipation, had taken their seats. A handful were already taking urgent notes.

"Their machine was radical," continued the young professor. "It was revolutionary, even scoffed at by some." The spirit in her voice was infectious and she sensed their budding anticipation. This was an important moment in the professional journey of these young men and women, and she would make it count. "But these two brothers, curious and innovative, would together change history like never before." She knew every line of her notes by heart, so her focus was on her audience. The students were captivated, almost spellbound, as she spoke. Julie paced the front of the room. Her aqua blue pants flowed freely over her legs, trim from long walks across the city. Her skin was golden from the summer sun and her brown hair, now long and well below her shoulders, stirred freely with her movement. "After weeks of delays from shattered propellers and a malfunctioning engine, the Wright Brothers were finally ready to create man's first powered flight." She smiled and it seemed the entire room followed suit.

The fall air was crisp and the first day of classes at the University of North Dakota had arrived on the campus with a keen eagerness. Julie Sampers, Associate Professor at the John D. Odegard School of Aerospace Science, stood in her lecture hall on the very western edge of the campus. Below the weather research satellite on top of the building and between two Air Traffic Control simulators, the 35-year-old junior college professor was beginning her second academic year in Lecture Hall 104.

"After flipping a coin, Orville climbed into their *Wright Flyer* to pilot the first powered aircraft in history." She smiled. "Facing frigid winds, gusting up to 27 miles per hour," she took a step forward, "the craft accelerated down their home-built ramp until it lifted into the air." Julie found it inspirational to reflect on humanity's first flight. After some of the most brilliant early minds in human history had pondered the possibility, the thought of two bicycle repairmen changing history stirred something in her. "In just twelve seconds," she stepped forward and everyone seemed to hold their breath. "Their airplane flew less than half the length of a football field at only seven miles per hour."

Julie was among the youngest academics in the department. Many educators at her age were flight instructing at the airport a few miles west of town, but her experience in the airlines and the moderate publicity she had received after safely landing an airplane after its captain became ill had earned her an interview. It was her passion that had gotten her the professorship. She had known before she was ten that she would be a pilot, but it had taken several years of flying for the airlines to realize teaching was her true calling.

"But the Wright Brothers were not the only American heroes to guide aviation's future," she paused with emphasis. Julie's principal method for assessing student engagement told her she had their attention: there was not a single student looking at their cell phone. "Though the US government was not quick to embrace aviation, independent inventors continued to push the limits of human flight."

It had been well over a decade since Julie had been a student at UND herself. Once she had completed her flight training and graduated, she had moved on to the airlines like so many of her peers. But now having been back in Grand Forks for just about a year, she had come to call it home again. She had walked the long city blocks in the summer and trekked the prairie in snowshoes through the winter. As she began to replant her roots in North Dakota, it was hard not to feel how much had changed since she was there as a student. Things were different now, not only in the city, but also within herself.

"Just over 20 years after the Wrights' maiden voyage, the next generation of pioneers quickly followed." The nerves of a new school year made it easy to capture an audience of freshmen students. "Charles Lindbergh, at only 25 years old, completed the first ever journey across the Atlantic Ocean in a single engine airplane." She paced across the room, her energy pulling the students' eyes. "James Doolittle, a PhD from M.I.T and a World War II hero, invented navigation technology airliners still use today." One student, who was wildly scribbling notes, stopped self-consciously when Julie paused in front of her desk. The professor gave her a reassuring smile and the student sat back in her chair. "Just 66 years after man's first flight, man journeyed to space." She eyed the room, taking slow and deliberate steps. "In a remarkable feat of human ingenuity, Neil Armstrong was the first human to walk on the Moon." Her voice slowed and the room was quiet. It was the first day of her Introduction to Aviation course and the seats were full of new students eager to begin their journey into aviation.

Intrepid Pursuit

"This is the history you are embarking on." She paused and studied the room. "You are entering a profession only 110 years in the making but advancing exponentially." She stood tall and let a smile pull the edge of her lips. "Perhaps some of you will fly the world's largest jumbo-jet." Her eyes connected with each student in the back row. "Maybe others will be a part of the return of the supersonic airliner." In all of her teaching, this was the moment she enjoyed the most. "Perhaps one of you will even be the first to walk on Mars."

Professor Julie Sampers was finding the magic that could change everything.

"Welcome to the University of North Dakota. When you leave here, you will be among the best pilots in the world." She paused, stepped behind the podium, and opened a textbook. "Now, let's get to work."

At the end of the hour, the students cleared the room. Some chatted nervously with Julie while she gathered her papers on the podium. She was buzzing with energy. Since the spring, she had been looking forward to today.

"You certainly know how to get their attention," said a man in the last row of the lecture hall. His redundant weight hardly fit into a single seat and it took him a moment to come to his feet. As the hall emptied, he made his way forward one step at a time. "You put on quite the introduction, professor," he smiled warmly.

Julie looked up, slightly startled, but was pleased when she recognized his familiar face. "I didn't see you up there, Ron!" She smiled and came forward.

"I wanted it that way," he said as his white sneakers settled on each step. "I've read all your glowing student reviews." He used the railing to steady himself on the final step. "I figured I'd have to see things for myself."

"It's so good to see you, Ron." She stepped in front of the podium and put her hand out. Instead, he extended his arms and wrapped them around her. "I cannot believe how quickly the summer has come and gone," she said, accepting his embrace.

Professor Ronald Rover was one of the most senior faculty members in the department. He was known both for his career as an aviator and academic, but also for his collection of colorful polos.

"The longer you teach, the faster they seem to go," he said, resting his hand on the podium. "I think you gave a fine introduction to these new students."

She laughed. "Teaching introduction courses makes you appreciate how much they will have to learn." Ron had become an unofficial mentor to Julie during the last academic school year. Thanks to his time and attention, Julie had grown both as a teacher and a person. She had always been one to keep to herself, but Ron was one of the few she didn't keep at arm's length. It was with Ron's support that Julie had found her place at the university.

She looked at her watch. There was a faculty meeting starting in a few minutes and she needed to run. She wanted to catch up with her mentor, talk about the summer that had come and gone, but she could not be late. Julie was the most junior member of the department and she had a lot of prove.

"I know you are busy," started Ron. He held his hands over his belly. "But I was hoping to catch you for just a moment."

Julie slid her bag over her shoulder. "Of course, Ron."

"I understand it is the very beginning of the year," he said, clearing his throat. He shifted his weight and Julie sensed him searching for the right words. "The chair approached me this morning," he continued. "He mentioned again that you didn't publish anything last year."

Speechless, Julie flinched. She wasn't even through the first day, and they had brought it up again. "I've just been focusing on my teaching and..." her voice trailed off.

"I understand," he smiled. He was nearing retirement and spoke with the casual tone of a professor in tenure. "I only tell you because other members of the faculty are talking about promotions and retention." Thankfully, he didn't feel the need to go on. Julie needed no reminder of the chorus "publish or perish" or her contract requiring publications each year. "They're already talking about who they will bring back again next year." He cleared his throat again. "I just thought you should know."

Julie exhaled. She didn't have much to say because it was true. Publications were part of her job, and she had produced nothing during her first year. Even when she had taken the position, she had known research wasn't her interest. The classroom was where she thrived. Sure, she could've been a flight instructor at the airport and skipped the academic busywork, but it would've kept her out of the lecture hall. She had spent her time in other ways last year, but clearly people were taking notice.

"Listen, I know research isn't your thing," Ron started. "In fact, it's tough for everyone." He laughed and Julie looked up. "I mention it to you so early because others will want more definitive answers soon."

"I'll figure something out." Julie said, feeling the weight of everything pressing down on her. If she didn't publish, she wouldn't have a job. It was as simple as that.

Outside, the campus was stirring with the energy of a new year. Classrooms were beginning to fill, and young pilots were learning to fly in the skies above.

"Julie," Ron started, giving her a knowing look. "You have a future here." He smiled. "This is a small bump in a long road."

Chapter 3

September 2024 | Hennepin County Medical Center
Minneapolis, Minnesota

"I presume the next of kin are on their way?" said the physician. In her long white lab coat, she flipped out her pager and fielded a message.

"They should be here in a few hours," said Frank Brewer tentatively. The concept of next of kin felt so cold, so detached that it made him uneasy. Given everything that happened, the idea made him even more tense. "The airline put them on the first plane to Minneapolis."

"Good," she said curtly. The Intensive Care Unit attending was short, but tall in presence. She had sharp features and eyes that were focused. "They'll want to be here."

"How is he doing?" asked Frank. He felt heavy and exhausted. A man accustomed to being in command, he was a fish out of water in this hospital. Worse, he felt responsible. He could only hope his stoicism would disguise everything going through his mind.

The physician flipped her pager closed and put it back in her coat pocket. They were standing in the hallway of the ICU, a busy place with alarms and hurried staff. To Frank, it was chaos. For the first time in his life, he tried to make himself smaller. "The family granted me permission to disclose his care to you," she said. A nurse hustled by with two IV poles while another tech wheeled a cart by.

Frank wore an oversized pair of sweats and a new pair of sneakers. The airline had given him the clothes because his bags had been left on the plane. On the surface it was a kind gesture, but he knew the real reason. They wanted to avoid him walking around the hospital in his company uniform. Frank had managed to get the airliner back to the runway seconds before the oxygen tanks had gone dry. Immediately, 155 people had been evacuated onto the runway. Most were loaded onto buses while others were rushed away in ambulances. Frank was somewhere in between. Despite the cough and the raging headache, he had ensured everyone on board was accounted for. He had finally agreed to be seen in the emergency department but had left it as soon as he could. Fortunately, most of his symptoms had abated now.

"Mr. Brewer," said the physician. Her beeper went off again, but she continued while she read the message. "Mr. Fischer has had several seizures." Frank frowned. "While he was in the ambulance, he stopped breathing." She looked up. "We had to place a breathing tube in his throat." Frank could feel the color draining from his face. While a dozen of his passengers were in the hospital, Cameron was by far the worst off. "He is stable now." The physician looked over her shoulder at the co-pilot in the room behind her. "Unfortunately, I am worried he has had a serious injury to his brain." A nurse put a clipboard in front of her and she signed it without a word. "The MRI will tell us more."

Frank nodded, dazed by the past few hours. In his 30 odd years as an airline pilot, he had never faced anything like this before. Even though late at night he'd sometimes feared it would come to this, he had ignored all the warnings. "How did this happen?" Frank asked. He knew the answer, but was hoping for anything else. This should never have happened. He could have stopped it.

"It's hard to say exactly," she said, holstering her pager again. Frank paid no attention to the bustle of the busy ICU. "Given ten other passengers have similar symptoms, we are suspicious there was a toxic exposure."

The words hit Frank like the crack of a bat.

William Hoffman

He had figured it would never happen to him because it was that unlikely. Of the thousands of flights every day, it had seemed impossible his would be the unlucky one. He didn't do anything wrong, per se, but he certainly hadn't done what was right either. He wasn't alone though; everyone kept quiet. It was an unspoken pact, and he had played his part in it.

"Given the signs," she continued, "slow heart rate, low blood pressure, and secretions, we are suspicious that the chemical had cholinergic activity."

"What the hell does that even mean?" Frank spat. It was all beginning to be too much. "Just be straight with me, doc. What happened?"

"Look," the doctor was unfazed, accustomed to defensive, angry reactions. "These people have been exposed to a toxin on your airplane." She emphasized the word "toxin" and Frank gritted his teeth. "We don't know what it was, but something serious happened here." Frank had questions, but he said nothing. And more than questions, he felt dread and guilt. "Now if you'll excuse me," said the physician. With a polite coldness, she clicked away in her black heels.

Chapter 4

September 2024 | Downtown
Grand Forks, North Dakota

The muffled rumble of a key passing through an old lock reverberated between the walls of the fourth-story apartment. Breathing heavily, Julie balanced the bag over her shoulder and the papers beneath her arm. She swung the door open and tossed the pile across the kitchen table, which was already stacked with journals and half-read books. A light mist dotted her forehead after her bike ride home in the evening humidity. The sun was less than an hour from falling below the horizon, but her workday was far from over. With her endless to-do list, her time at home tended to be the most productive. Her body felt heavy from a long first day, but she was not ready to rest. A new school year was always frenetic, but Julie had always found it energizing.

Kicking off her shoes, she sat on the couch. Her apartment was small, with worn wooden floors and holes in the sheetrock, but it was home. Since her lecture this morning, Professor Rover's words had been weighing on her mind. There was something about teaching that seemed to bring out the best in her. Though the work was never-ending, it was compelling and it challenged her. If she wanted to stay, she would have to fight. Certainly, it would not be the first time that she had fought for something.

William Hoffman

```
Altitude induced hypoxia and metabolic capacity of
             the semicircular canals.
```

A stack of papers sat on her coffee table and she eyed them timidly. It was research Ron had encouraged her to take on the previous year but that she had avoided. Honestly, it was dreadful, and she sought any reason to stay away from it. Despite weighing on her all summer, the work had been untouched for months.

A movement in the corner of her apartment grabbed her attention.

"Come here, Amelia!" Julie's voice was high and gentle. She rubbed her hand on the sofa. The cat jumped on the couch and flicked her tail curiously. A scratch made the cat's arch grow higher and Julie smiled. Amelia, named after the first woman pilot to fly across the Atlantic Ocean, was a good companion in her quiet life in North Dakota. Despite having grown up in the rural hills of West Virginia, this was her home now. She had flown out of Seattle for a budget airline for a few years after college but was glad to be back. While some days she missed her life as an airline pilot, being settled was a treat. A childhood of trials and reactive moves had made her self-reliant. *"You listen to me, Julie,"* her father had said with a belly full of whiskey. He had stumbled and pointed at Julie while she waited in the doorway with her school bookbag. *"You're just a little rat."* The accent of the Blue Ridge mountains had always come out when he was drunk. Her escape had seemed like a miracle and to go to college even more so. She had sworn she would never go back and had kept her promise. Her four years as a student at UND had been the longest she had ever lived in a single city. It was a place where no one knew the demons of her past and she could be whoever she wanted. She was free and had learned early on that privacy was a powerful defense.

On the couch, Julie picked up the first 100 pages and leafed through the documents. Eyeing the pile, she exhaled. She was a teacher, not a researcher, but knowing what was on the line made it all even more unnerving. This project felt unimportant and like a distraction from the work that really mattered. She closed her eyes, palming her forehead in her hand. At this university and with these students was where she belonged. Despite it all, she'd have to fight if she wanted to stay. Adjusting the stack, she took the first page and began to read again.

```
Aircraft operational altitude poses an occupational
risk for aircraft crew and passengers. High
functioning aircraft often have a pressurization
system that will increase the perceived cabin
pressure for comfort and physiologic function...
```

Buzz.

It was her cell phone and she quickly pulled it out.

RYAN RIFE @ 2049: `Happy first day! Let's get a drink.`

The message spurred a tickle in her stomach. She read it again, her smile cutting deeper. Julie typed her response, knowing there were few people in the world who could bring her to leave unfinished work so easily.

Julie Sampers @ 2050: `Meet me at Brick and Barley at 9. :)`

The sun had fallen below the horizon and the cool Dakota air was crisp. A trailer loaded with sugar beets passed slowly along Demers Avenue and a bank was locking its doors for the night. Walking into the quiet Monday night bar, Julie was a little nervous. Ryan was an instructor pilot at the airport and several years her junior. They'd met at a work function early last year and had become some sort of friends. They hadn't seen each other since the previous school year but their spring together had been one Julie could not forget. Her anticipation grew, thinking of all the possibilities. A lifetime of lessons had taught her to be cautious, to be guarded, but there was something different about Ryan. He was sensitive and kind. With him, she sensed the kind of comfort for which she longed.

"Back here!" said Ryan waving his hand. He was sitting alone at a corner table. His smile was warm and his eyes bright. Dimples cut into his cheeks, a feature that always drew Julie's eyes. On the chest of his pressed white shirt, a UND logo was embroidered in green. He had come right from the airport after instructing in one of the University's training airplanes. "With a smile like that, it must've been a good day," he said.

"Something like that." She boosted herself into a stool across the table. Two glasses of amber IPA sat cold and ready. "I could sure use one of these, though." Ryan laughed while Julie hid her smile in the foam. The Monday night bar was quiet, with a few regulars hunched over the bar, and a table of students near the front door. The refrain of an Eric Church song played quietly over muffled chatter and the smell of spilled beer.

"We're anxiously waiting for those freshmen to hit the airport," he said. Ryan was tall and trim, with the build of a lifelong runner. He wore his certainty easily and his gaze drew Julie in. Everything that had happened last spring came back to Julie in an instant. The laughter to tears, the late-night conversations, and the romance played like a chorus in her mind. While spending time with Ryan, Julie had discovered so much about herself. Their times together had been infrequent, thanks to two busy schedules, but Julie didn't need much. It had been about the quality, not quantity. She had initially been careful about the whole thing, hesitant about what she felt. But through every moment, Ryan had guided her by the hand. Much more was felt than said but Julie could tell how strong her feelings were. They didn't talk about their pasts, in fact Julie knew very little about Ryan beyond his work. The details didn't matter because their connection was all about the present.

It had been a few months into the spring semester when they had acted on their lust. It had been cathartic, leaving her with emotions unlike she had felt before. Together they had stepped forward into the unknown, but it wasn't frightening with Ryan. The feelings were complex, and the future uncertain, but Ryan seemed to understand her like no one else.

"How was Phoenix?" Julie asked, feeling the press of anticipation. At the end of last year, Ryan had mentioned he would be spending the summer at the university's sister campus in Arizona to flight instruct for a few months. He'd assured her it wouldn't be long, and he would be back in the fall, but Julie had taken the news hard. Even though their time together had been brief, it was a gift. When Ryan had left in May, Julie had assumed they would stay as close. Unfortunately, it hadn't been the case. The distance between them had been a difficult obstacle and they had grown apart. The sudden change had left Julie feeling vulnerable and heavy with questions. Despite the grief, she said nothing. After all, what could she expect? She had made it clear that she valued her freedom and Ryan, who was discreet and private in his own way, never needed an explanation.

"It was hot," he said with an easy laugh. Julie settled into a familiar warmth she had missed. "But it sure was fun." His head tilted slightly to the side and the darks of his eyes pulled Julie. "I just got back last night, actually."

"You don't waste any time," said Julie. She stirred in her seat. "And you flew today?"

"Of course, I did!" he smiled. "You know I love it." He threw down the last of his beer and looked back at Julie. Blushing, she looked at her hands.

"You're going to have to slow down at some point," Julie said. For a moment, it felt like they hadn't missed any time at all. "That smile of yours is going to wear down." She looked up.

"I'm always smiling when I'm with you." At 29 years old, he was among the top flight instructors in the department. The years of age between them felt inconsequential. If anything, it made it more interesting.

After their second IPA, the laughter came easier. They exchanged stories and talked about old times. The time passed quickly and Julie didn't want it to end. All the questions that Julie had once had seemed unimportant because he was here with her now.

"Did you hear what happened in Minneapolis today?" Ryan asked. He waved down the bartender for a third round. "Another Avionica Airlines airplane had an emergency landing." Empty tables around them began to fill in. "I guess it filled with smoke."

"Another airplane?" Julie said distractedly. Frankly, she was more interested in making up for lost time than the news.

"Over the past year, I guess they've had three airplanes make emergency landings because of smoke filling the cabin," he said.

"I hadn't heard anything about it," Julie said. She usually watched the news headlines, looking for topics to bring up in class, but this was new. She knew little about Avionica other than their hefty profits and cramped cabins.

"They do a good job of keeping it quiet," Ryan said. The waiter brought another pair of full mugs and gathered the empties. "It doesn't usually make it into the news, but it seemed to this time."

"And how do you know about this?" she asked. She took a sip of beer, not looking away.

"I hear all the airline gossip," he winked. He leaned forward, his eyes bringing Julie closer.

"I don't doubt it," she said. "It seems like you're always up to something."

"I have friends who are pilots for Avionica. They told me people are in the hospital."

"People got hurt?" asked Julie, sitting back in her chair. She was surprised that she had not heard about it.

"Seven people went to the hospital," Ryan said. A group of students rolled in through the door of the bar while another table burst into laughter. "Including the copilot, who happens to be a UND grad." The music was turned up louder and a table across the bar cheered. "The whole thing is strange."

At the end of the night, Julie and Ryan stood outside on the quiet city street, lined with old buildings from another time. The yellow hue of the streetlights illuminated a handful of people ambling along the quiet Monday night sidewalks. Bakers would be filing into *Great Harvest Bread* two doors down in a few hours and the new Grand Forks Brewery stood ready for another day of production.

Ryan's hands were tucked into the pockets of his uniform, hiding from the cool breeze. His uniform was untucked, and his tie loosened. A playful laugh was dissipating after a story from days gone by as the summer air swirled between them.

"It was good to see you, Ryan," She looked up to him, her lips smiling and full. Ryan took a step forward. As they moved closer, Julie's breathing deepened. There was a pause and then a nervous laugh.

"Are we back here again?" he asked. Ryan pushed a strand of hair behind her ear.

"If you want to be." She let her hands fall to her sides. "We can be."

"It was hard to be away from you this summer, Julie."

"I missed you," she said. Julie held her breath, feeling her heart in her chest. There was so much she wanted to say but didn't need to. She had never felt this way about someone else before, she was sure of it. She had tried to deny it when she was alone this summer, but seeing him again only reaffirmed what she already knew.

Ryan smiled and exhaled. He reached his hand to Julie's and time seemed to slow. They looked into each other's eyes and something pulsed between them. Letting herself be guided by the hand, they walked north along the train tracks towards her apartment. Tonight, they'd be making up for lost time.

Chapter 5

September 2024 | Hennepin County Medical Center
Minneapolis, Minnesota

In the baggy cloth of his grey sweat suit, Captain Frank Brewer paced the waiting room of the Hennepin County Medical Center Intensive Care Unit. With his gaze on the floor, he moved urgently. His fingers were interlaced behind his back, and his thoughts distant. At nearly two in the morning, the cold fluorescent lights showed every line etched into his face.

Frank had spent the day watching his co-pilot lying in a hospital bed. He thought how helpless the twenty-something year old with tubes pumping in and out of his fragile body looked. Cameron was just a kid, a nice kid at that, but he was now completely dependent on the nurses caring for him. His decline since that morning was unsettling and Frank couldn't sit. Cameron's parents were still on their way, but wouldn't make it to the hospital until the red-eye from Tampa landed in the morning. He couldn't just leave Cameron all alone in this place. Not after knowing everything that happened. Frank paused, looking at the clock for a moment, and paced the room again.

"Frank," a tall man walked into the waiting room. He spoke with a graveled inflection. The man's grey hair was cut short, like a military buzz, and a neatly trimmed mustache hung over his mouth. His black airline captain suit was well cut, and he held a leather briefcase at his side.

Frank turned to face the pilot, not saying anything. Fatigue pulled at his eyes as he stood there. He had been expecting this visit, but it didn't make it any easier. Frank's jaw tightened and he lifted his chin, waiting for the man to say something.

"It was nice of you to stay, Frank." The airline captain took two cautious steps into the waiting room. He eyed the space to make sure all the seats were empty. "You didn't have to do that." He placed his briefcase on a seat and closed the door behind him.

"Of course I did, Jett," the words came harsh and fast. "I couldn't leave this kid here by himself after all of this." The uniformed pilot wore a pair of clear-rimmed glasses that somehow seemed to highlight the silver hair above his mouth. He was surprised by Frank's tone but didn't flinch. There was silence while each waited for the other to play his hand.

"Look, I tried to come here earlier," Jett said, breaking his glance. "I was dealing with something else in Chicago." He inched forward, but no more than a step. "I got here as fast as I could."

"It doesn't matter how fast you got here, Jett," Frank shot back. He remained unmoving, his hands still behind his back. "The damage is already done."

Jett scratched his chin, apparently buying time. Frank could tell the senior pilot was thinking hard but knew there wasn't much to say. The pause was long but Frank didn't budge. He'd submitted too many times before, and there was no way in hell he was about to do it again.

"Look, Frank, I know today has been tough…" Jett hesitated.

"Don't give me that shit, Jett," Frank shot back. A nurse passed the window and he lowered his voice. "*You* let it happen." He let his hands fall to his sides.

"This could've been anything, Frank," said Jett cautiously. He held his palms forward, hoping things would slow down.

William Hoffman

"Bullshit!" Frank interjected. He took a step forward, his mind accelerating. He'd always been a loyal member of this company, but things had gone too far. Frank saw a familiar pain in the man's eyes. "We flew together for years," Frank said, his tone changing. He looked to Jett, searching for anything rational in all this madness. "We were friends, Jett," he begged. "How could you let this happen?" The uniformed pilot looked away. "Don't think that just because you're the chief pilot now that it means you can lie to me."

"We won't know what's happened until there is an investigation." Captain Jett Fitzgerald's voice slowed, almost like he had realized it was the wrong thing to say before he made it to the end of his sentence. For a moment, Frank wondered if Jett also felt the heaviness, the guilt of knowing.

"You and I both know exactly what has happened here, Jett." Frank pointed at the floor. The guilt was cultivating into anger. "Now we have this kid," he pointed to the hospital room, "with a tube down his throat because of the decisions your people made." His voice grew louder again, riled by Jett's unbothered eyes.

"Frank, please," Jett took another step forward. Frank wasn't naïve; he knew it always came back to the money. Jett had made his allegiance clear long ago but until today, Frank hadn't realized the price Jett was willing to pay.

"No Jett, I won't!" he remained unmoved. He was tired and had had enough. The grey shadows beneath his eyes had been cast by years of red-eye flights, sleep deprivation, and the burden of a captain's responsibility. He could tolerate the long days and the short nights. He hadn't had more than a few days off in months. He had put up with the old airplanes and the leadership turnover, but he wouldn't put up with shortcuts. Not when this was what it meant. At least, not anymore.

Standing under the cold lights of the intensive care unit, he knew the reason why this cut so deep. This was his fault too. He had heard what was going on - the hushing, the close calls, the risk - but he had kept it to himself. It didn't have anything to do with him, so he remained quiet – just like the company wanted. He was an accomplice in it all. Now with his passengers in the hospital and his co-pilot in the ICU, he wouldn't keep quiet any longer.

Intrepid Pursuit

"You know exactly what happened here," spat Frank. Jett remained silent, looking away. This time it was different, and he would not let it end this way. "And it's been going on for *years*."

Now, it was personal.

Chapter 6

September 2024 | Downtown
Grand Forks, North Dakota

The morning sun eased through the curtains, pulling Julie from sleep. The crisp fall breeze filled her bedroom with a soothing coolness. As the cloak of sleep fell, Julie realized she was smiling. Propping herself up in bed, she stretched her arms and heard Amelia's call for breakfast. Alone, she looked for evidence of the previous night. Her bed was empty, but there was something on the pillow. She unfolded the paper and read it twice.

```
Thanks for the drink. Off to the airport.
```

Falling back into the blankets, Julie smiled again.

Ryan made her feel unlike anything she had felt before. When they had grown apart so easily over the summer, she had felt vulnerable and alone. Wounds from her earlier life had been torn open and she had cursed herself for bringing down her defenses. But now that they were together again, she mused on everything that seemed possible. She wondered if this feeling, one she had never put into words, was love. Even better, maybe Ryan felt it too.

It was just after nine when Julie was sitting at her desk on the third floor of Odegard Hall. Her office was small, with white walls, and oppressive fluorescent lights that cast deep shadows. She had a single desk, on which her laptop was plugged in, and some potted plants beside a window. It wasn't much, but it was enough. She pulled out her phone, hoping for a message from Ryan, but there was nothing. Instead, she thought of their conversation last night and opened a web browser.

```
Google.com
```

```
                [ENTER]
```

There was something about what Ryan had said about that flight yesterday that had stuck with her. She wondered about the story behind how something like this could happen three times in the same year.

```
"Avionica Minneapolis emergency"
```

```
                [ENTER]
```

The Google results populated the screen, and she browsed the text.

"Avionica Airlines flight returns to MSP after mysterious smoke puts nine in the hospital."

Julie bit her lip. She clicked the link and skimmed the first few lines.

> Nine people are in the hospital, one in critical condition, after an Avionica Airlines A320 departed from Minneapolis-St. Paul International Airport on Tuesday for a routine flight to Tampa, Florida. According to passenger reports, a "white smoke" filled the cabin followed by a "chemical odor," causing coughing and respiratory distress.

She set her coffee cup down and leaned forward. Weather or a routine mechanical issue could bring an airliner back, but something about this seemed different. She continued to scroll.

> Moments after take-off, oxygen masks were deployed, and the aircraft made a steep bank back to the airport. Ill passengers were taken to Hennepin County Medical Center in Minneapolis by ambulance after an emergency landing.

Julie mumbled to herself, focused on the page. When she was still flying, they had prepared for many things. Engine failures and fire training were routine, but this was something different. A mysterious gas filling the cabin was entirely new to her. Her curiosity stirred and her thoughts accelerated. Droves of explanations could possibly account for fog in an airliner, but only a few toxic enough to put someone in the hospital.

> While the airline has made no statement, the National Transportation Safety Board said it would investigate. More information will be released as it becomes available.

"Good morning!" said Professor Rover, appearing in the doorway. She hadn't seen him coming so she jumped. "Did you have a good ride in?" he asked. He supported himself on the doorframe and rested a steaming cup of coffee on his belly.

"Oh," Julie said. "Hi Ron." She turned towards the door, trying to clear the clouds.

"Listen," he took a step into the room and he lowered his voice. "About yesterday…" he paused. Julie could sense he'd been thinking about it. "Maybe I shouldn't have dropped that bombshell on you after your lecture," he said. "I know it's the first week of school and…" There was a pause while both looked for the words.

"I know you're just looking out for me," she said with a half-hearted smile. Ron looked relieved. She waved for him to come in and take a seat. "I actually started looking at some stuff yesterday." She felt the weight of her academic responsibility again. If she wanted to stay, she needed a plan.

"Don't tell me it's that semicircular canal project," said Ron playfully. He took a sip of coffee. "There's a reason why you stopped it last year." Julie appreciated Ron's mentorship, but even more so, she was grateful for the father figure that he had slowly become.

"It is dreadful..." Julie admitted. Ron bellied a laugh, and she followed.

"We'll find you something, Julie," he said after another sip. "We just have to find something that interests you."

She sat forward, looking back at her computer. "What do you make of this flight in Minneapolis?" she asked, turning the screen towards him. Ron flipped out a pair of glasses and perched them on his nose.

"Avionica is at it again," he said after skimming the page. Unmoved, he sat back in his chair. His comment took her by surprise. Julie hadn't heard much about the company beyond their dismal customer service and cheap tickets. She had booked a last-minute weekend get-away on Avionica the previous year and had found that they lived up to their poor reputation. "Every few years I hear something about Avionica," he said. "It's a fascinating company, to be honest."

"What kind of stuff are you talking about?" She thought about Ryan's comment last night, wondering what they both knew that she did not.

"Every year or two you hear about an airplane full of smoke. Never usually makes it into the news, I'll tell you that much." He adjusted in his seat. "They are very good at keeping things like that quiet."

"You think they're hiding something?" Intrigued, she leaned forward and began picking at her thumbnail.

"Avionica is an airline that makes money on shortcuts," he said. Two faculty members walked by the open office door. "And not shortcuts between cities." He chuckled.

"I haven't heard anything about this," she said.

"Their CEO was asked why their service was so bad at a news conference a few years ago," Ron continued. Julie had realized early on that much of what made Ron an exceptional teacher was that he was a storyteller. "He responded by asking why they would change anything if profits were growing so rapidly!'"

"What kind of things are they trying to cover up?" Julie asked.

"In the early days of airlines using jet engines, there were reports of toxic fumes filling airplane cabins." He spun the cup in his hand. "It was new because it had never happened in propeller driven airplanes. The whole thing was quite interesting."

"I have never heard of any of else," Julie said.

"They called it 'Aerotoxic Syndrome' and the industry worked quietly to clean things up." Julie looked on, her mind piecing it together. "There were fewer airlines back then, and the story is that they came together to find a quiet fix

"You mean to tell me the FAA didn't investigate something like that?" Julie could hardly believe it. With a safety record like the US aviation system, it seemed impossible for something like this to be ignored. "You can't think this is still happening."

"Congress commissioned an investigation, but nothing came of it." He gave her a knowing smile. "One airline figured out a fix and the others seemed to fall in line." He paused. "Except, maybe, for Avionica, of course."

"If that is still happening, it would be in the news," she protested. She usually prided herself on keeping on the pulse of the industry. "How have I not heard about this before?"

"Like I said," Ron pushed off his armrests and rose to his feet. His coffee cup was empty and hanging down by his side. "They make money on shortcuts," he said. "And their influence is wide." He started towards the door.

"What are they hiding?" Julie asked, intrigued, and wanting more.

Ron smiled. "It looks like we found you a topic." When he was at the door, she came to her feet. "Perhaps there's a story to be told here, Julie," he said. "Something more to be discovered."

Julie paused, considering it all. "Where would I even start on something like that?" She was still picking at her thumbnail.

"Didn't that article say there's a pilot in the hospital down there?" Ron pointed to the laptop and Julie's eyes followed. "He probably has some ideas." With a warm smile, he winked. "Perhaps you should get yourself down to Minneapolis."

Outside the door of lecture hall 104, Julie unlocked her phone. The lecture was due to start in a minute and over 100 freshman students were waiting for her. Julie was ready, but she needed to do one thing first.

```
und.edu/flight-operations
```

                                          `[ENTER]`

      'Reserve an Aircraft'

                                          `[ENTER]`

If she was going to get to Minneapolis tonight, she'd have to fly.

Chapter 7

September 2024 | Avionica Airlines Headquarters
Tampa Bay, Florida

Four grey spires pierced the humid air under the oppressive Tampa sun. The ashen building was 50 stories high, with small windows that made it hard to not only gaze in, but also out. The concrete structure soaked the staggering September heat in and held it tight.

Under the vaulted awning of the building's entrance, men and women in suits walked hastily amid fountains and chauffeured Cadillacs. People spoke in hushed tones or simple nods. A taxi pulled up beneath the awning, where two women were fanning themselves with a copy of the *Tampa Bay Times*. The front-page story had spurred chatter on every floor of the skyscraper that towered over East Whiting Street.

Above the 50th floor, three massive flags were mounted. They waved freely so they could be seen from any point around the fortress. One flag, slightly lower than the other two, displayed the red and white colors of the flag of Florida. To its left, the stars and stripes of the American flag were waving in the wind. The final flag, displayed on the far-right side, moved more slowly in the air. One could not help but notice it was not only larger than the other two, but also slightly higher. The flag was yellow, one color from top to bottom, with a simple black seal. In bold letters, two words could be read from the streets below.

Avionica Airlines

On the top floor, a packed boardroom was in silence. The 15 people occupying lush leather chairs were waiting anxiously around a mahogany table. Their hair was mostly grey, but all their suits were black. One woman shuffled through a stack of papers while others stared at steaming cups of coffee. Their nervous energy required no more caffeine.

A man finally broke the silence. "We don't know what this is about." He pulled off his glasses and wiped the beads of sweat from his forehead. From floor to ceiling, the vaulted windows displayed the rolling waves of the Atlantic Ocean on the beaches beside the city. It was an uncomfortable backdrop to the tension between the executives. "This could be anything, let's just see what he says."

Across the table, no one said a word. In fact, no one dared to even look his way. The only response was the sound of breathing and throat clearing. He recoiled nervously.

They had all received the message two hours before. After frantic texts and hurried travel, they had all found themselves here, unready to face whatever had triggered this meeting. From the deck of his luxurious beach chateau, airline owner Bruce Luxton had called an emergency board meeting. The text was simple, and there was no need for questions. Now, he was on his personal jet heading north from the Cayman Islands. The Gulfstream G-650 twin engine business jet was cutting through the salty ocean air at a speed approaching its maximum.

Opposite the man, a woman finally spoke. "Of course we know what this is about, Michael." She had short hair and a red blouse beneath her blazer. "We should have a plan before he arrives." She spoke almost in a whisper, which triggered a cascade of shifting and murmurs.

William Hoffman

Michael Burben didn't move. At the end of the table, he felt small. He thought about how much he had given, how much he had sacrificed, and he wondered if it was all about to be lost. He knew he was vulnerable in his post. Over the past five years, three people had sat in his chair and he wondered how long it would be until he became the fourth. Since he had become vice president of Avionica Airlines six months earlier, dark shadows had grown under his eyes. He had lost weight amid the stress, and his marriage, which had already been on the rocks, hadn't survived the first few months. The challenge had been compelling at first, the power intoxicating, but it had come at a cost. The money and luxuries were endless, but it was taking everything he had. Now, propped up like a marionette, he felt empty. He knew that the man he feared most was hurtling over the ocean directly toward him at over 500 miles per hour.

"Let's see what he has to say," said Vice President Michael Burben. He tried to sound calm, not sure if he was reassuring his subordinates or himself. "It could be anything.

Chapter 8

September 2024 | Flying Cloud Airport
Eden Prairie, Minnesota

Just before eight, the hind wheels of the white and green Cessna 172 with the university seal on its tail kissed the asphalt at Flying Cloud Airport. The trainer turned off the main runway as the evening sun painted the horizon in stunning shades. The airport was among the busiest in the metro, but tonight it was quiet. Usually, medical choppers and executive flights kept the airport busy, but the field was Julie's alone tonight.

"Sioux 6645 turn right on echo 2 taxiway and taxi to general aviation parking," said the air traffic controller over the radio. Every airplane in the university fleet held the callsign, a nod to the former "Fighting Sioux" mascot. After the National College Athletic Association had required a name change in 2015, fans now cheered for the "Fighting Hawks", but 110,000 yearly training flights retained their original callsign. Julie confirmed the direction and navigated the field. At the small terminal building, she flipped off the engine and popped the door open. After three hours in the air, the fuel tanks were nearly empty, but her bladder was full.

Flying over the prairie, her mind had replayed Ron's words. Flocks of geese had soared over the marshes while she cruised just below the clouds. Despite the view, she had been distracted. Flying across the state on a whim felt crazy, perhaps even irrational, but something was pulling at her. It was possible it was all nothing, but Ron had spiked her curiosity. The idea that something sinister was lurking in plain sight seemed impossible. Millions of people fly every day without an issue and for good reason. The US aviation system is a model for safety across the globe. But no matter how she tried to rationalize it, there was something that didn't seem to add up. Beyond publishing and defending her job, she wondered if there could really be something bigger going on.

In the cockpit, she gathered her things. With the parking brake on, she stashed her headset and maps into her bag. She also took a stack of papers from the backseat and carefully slid them into her backpack. It was possible they were a key to this puzzle, and she wanted to keep them close. After her morning lecture, her teaching assistant had apologized for missing the first day of class, although based on his swim shorts and flip-flops, she had deduced he wasn't intending to stay long today either.

"There is actually one thing you can help me with," she had told the TA as the classroom emptied. "Go to the library." She tore a page out of her notebook and began writing. "Get me every article you can find on Aerotoxic Syndrome." The light faded from the senior aviation student's eyes as she passed him the list. "Can you get this to me in a few hours?"

"Well, I..." his voice trailed off. "I suppose I could."

"If you do this for me now," she smiled, "I don't imagine you'll need to come to this lecture for the next month or two."

"Awesome!" he said, perking up and hustling off to the library. A few hours later, he had brought back a stack of articles taller than Julie had anticipated, but she hadn't been deterred. She intended to read every word of it.

After a quick pit stop in the terminal, she headed for the parking lot. It was empty apart from a single car at the back of the lot. Flying Cloud was a favorite stop for many reasons, and one was the free courtesy car the airport kept for pilots. It wasn't fancy, but it was available. Julie grabbed the keys and tossed her bags in the back. But before she put it into drive, she paused. Alongside the excitement of the afternoon, something else was weighing on her mind.

Ryan.

Still swimming in all the feelings that the day before had brought, Julie couldn't help but smile. Beyond lust, there was something more. She was surprised by how quickly she'd fallen back into this warm swirl of romance. Sure, they had often discussed the value they both placed on their independence but seeing Ryan again had felt different. Julie had tried so hard to move on when they had been apart in the summer, but it now seemed clear to her that Ryan wanted to pick up from where they had left off. Julie wanted nothing more. It was just a little odd that Ryan hadn't responded to her message yet. She had texted him in the morning and hadn't heard back. In the car, she checked her phone again. Still no message. She felt a little silly for hovering over her phone like this, but it seemed unlike him. He was usually quick with a witty reply, but he hadn't said a word all day.

```
Hennepin County Medical Center, Minneapolis, MN
```

Julie entered the destination in her GPS and started the car. She exhaled, trying to relax a little. Growing up with a painful family past had taught her lessons she could not forget. Too many times, she had been reminded to only trust herself. She had constructed a tall, deep wall around her, one that had protected her from outsiders. Though there was often loneliness at its center, it was safe. But Ryan made her want to change that. He showed her that more was possible. He could teach her a different way to build, to deconstruct the barrier around her, and create something new. At least, that's what Julie was hoping for. As she drove highway 494 heading north towards downtown Minneapolis, Julie could think of little else.

Buzz.

It was a text. Julie's stomach tickled. She turned into the Hennepin County Medical Center parking garage and put the car in park. Holding her breath, she finally read his message.

RYAN RIFE @ 2022: There is something you should know. I haven't been completely honest with you.

Chapter 9

September 2024 | Avionica Airlines Headquarters
Tampa Bay, Florida

The department leaders from across Avionica Airlines fidgeted uneasily in their seats. Around the boardroom table, time was slow. Outside, waves fell onto the beaches below, where tourists played freely in the salty air. Their calm was at complete odds with the apprehension in the boardroom. The executives' focus was on the double doors near the head of the table.

No one shifted in their seats more than Michael Burben. He took a sip of water, but it rolled over his tongue like oil. When he finally managed to get it down his throat, he felt sick. The only thing he needed right now was for all of this to be over. The vice president's eyes studied the unlikely group of people. Each had fought their way to a seat at this table. Many had been poached from other industries, having proven their worth through ruthless means. Their merciless tactics were reflected in growing stocks and ballooning profits. The executives were highly compensated by the private, low-budget airline. Though their salaries were easily double their industry peers, Michael knew too well that it came at a price. To be at the head of this table was what he had always wanted. For years, he had fought to get here. Now, he did not know what he wanted. Even if it was this, he was not sure how much longer he could take it.

His Blackberry vibrated in his pocket and he fumbled to fish it out. Every eye in the room turned to him. It was a message from his assistant.

Cynthia @ 1301: `He's here`.

Michael felt his abdomen squeeze. He had an urge to flee, but he knew there was no place to run to.

"Luxton is here," he said quietly.

Like fawns in the woods, no one dared move. Michael should have been ready, he knew that. It was his job to have a plan. When things went wrong, he was supposed to fix it. That was the deal when he agreed to take this job. He had always considered himself to be among the best, but this place was making him question everything. He was not ready. In fact, he was completely empty-handed. Now, he could only wait for what was to come.

The double doors swung open. The wood collided with the walls like a gunshot.

"What is going on here, Burben!" Bruce Luxton strode into the room with his fists clenched. The airline owner was a tall man, with jet-black hair and swollen pectoral muscles that bulged below his shirt. No one dared blink, let alone move. Mr. Luxton pressed his fists into the head of the table. "I presume you saw the news this morning?" His colorful board shorts were in stark contrast to the suits of his uneasy employees. He could conduct company business in flip-flops and Ray-Bans because every penny of this $700 million company belonged to him.

Michael's heart was clapping at the bottom of his throat when he came to his feet. He could only get out single syllable noises and no one at the table offered help.

"Get it out, Burben!" Luxton spat.

"Sir, we are aware of the situation," Michael managed. Nausea began to heap.

"You better be more than just aware." There was a collective recoil. Michael had seen his boss upset before, but not like this. "Do you have any idea what this could mean for this company?" Luxton's feverish stare assaulted the room.

"Yes, sir," Michael coughed. "Absolutely, sir."

"You have one job," he said. A vein on his forehead pulsed. "Keep airplanes moving," he pointed at Burben, "and make this company money."

"Yes, sir," Michael leaned forward, clawing for composure. "We have a plan, sir." He prayed the lie would hold.

"There'd better be more than just a plan." Luxton leaned over the head of the table. "You and I *both* know what will happen if this gets out. Do you understand?" The VP tried to concur but was cut off. Luxton repeated his question louder.

"We know exactly what you mean, sir," Michael said. "We will get things settled." Michael squinted his eyes, feeling his external shield failing. He was aching for a drink. After today, maybe the bottle would be the only thing he had left.

Luxton turned away and exhaled. He rubbed his eyes, clearly thinking through it all. In the ocean beyond, clouds began to fill the sky and wind brought white caps to the waves. When Luxton turned back towards Michael, his expression had changed. Where there had been only anger, there was now also a hint of fear.

"If I go to prison," Luxton started. He took a step towards Michael, nearly whispering. "I'm not going alone."

Chapter 10

September 2024 | Hennepin County Medical Center
Minneapolis, Minnesota

The hospital was quiet this time of evening. A handful of nurses were chatting near the entry doors while a man wearing earplugs polished floors. The vaulted lobby looked like it was from another time, with ceilings and floors nearly the same shade of beige. The coffee corral was closed, and the information desk was vacant. Walking through the sliding doors, Julie felt like she didn't belong. Her body stiffened, and she walked in a mechanical way, trying to blend in. Even in the empty lobby, it felt like all eyes were on her.

The hospital complex expanded over multiple city blocks, connected by skyways over city streets. There were hundreds of patient rooms and thousands of people. Already, the search felt futile. Passing by signs and waiting areas, she rebuked herself for not having had a clear plan. She suddenly felt naive for thinking she could find this pilot without something to go on. As she walked further into the lobby, something dawned on her: a simple question that had not occurred to her until now. What would she even ask this pilot if she found him? There were the obvious ones, but it felt so clumsy. Honestly, the whole thing felt a little foolish. Doubt pulled her back towards the door, but something also kept her moving forward.

The closed information desk was on the far side of the lobby, beside a bank of elevators. The computer was dark, and the chair was empty. But beside the stacks of pamphlets, something caught her eye. She cut across the lobby, looking over her shoulder. On top of the counter, there was a basket. Inside, there were name tags.

Guest

Julie could hardly believe they were left unguarded, but it wasn't the time to ask questions. She grabbed one off the top and fled towards a bank of elevators. She clicked the button, the bell rang, and she disappeared behind the doors. After rereading the news article this morning, at least she knew which floor to start on.

```
           4ᵀᴴ Floor
      INTENSIVE CARE UNIT
```

She began picking her thumbnail with her teeth. With each floor, the elevator bell rang. Her analytical side was begging her to consider what she was doing, but intrigue was urging her forward. *There's a story to be told here, Julie.* It felt crazy; she would admit that, but she had already come this far. Why not see what she could find?

Ascending on the elevator, Julie thought of the people who had been trapped inside that airplane as it filled with smoke. The panic would be overwhelming, and people would be praying for their lives. Perhaps, some of them still were. It would be a nightmare, but apparently not the first one. Not only had Professor Ron Rover known the curious history of this company, but so had Ryan. *I have not been completely honest with you.* The reminder of Ryan stung, and Julie still felt dazed. She had been trying to push him out of her mind since she landed, but it was a hopeless effort. In the parking lot of Flying Cloud Airport, Julie had responded to his message.

JULIE SAMPERS @ 2023: `What's going on?`

William Hoffman

Her mind was racing with questions. It started with uncertainty, but shame about her feelings quickly followed. To make it worse, Ryan hadn't responded. Again, he went silent.

On the fourth floor of the hospital, the elevator doors opened. Julie stepped out onto the corridor, adjusting the backpack higher on her shoulder, and looked around warily. *I haven't been completely honest with you.* Despite her caution, she had let her guard down for Ryan. She had trusted him so quickly but now couldn't help but wonder if it had been a mistake. She felt uneasy thinking about all the things she could not control, but at least here in this hospital she could choose her next step forward.

The corridors and hallways reflected the Hennepin County Medical Center's history: over 100 years of additions, construction, and change. Just six blocks from the Minneapolis U.S. Bank Football stadium, it was the sole level one trauma center and safety net hospital in the city. Halfway down the first hallway, she tried to blend in among the shuffle of nurses and visitors. Two physicians, a man and a woman, chatted casually as they passed. There was a nursing unit on her right and an empty waiting room on her left. The sterile smell of chemical cleaner swirled in her nose as she hunted for a sign to the ICU. As she passed by another unit and a set of doors, something caught her eye. It was curious and stopped her in place.

There was a pilot in the hospital. Not an ill one, but one in uniform.

He was walking along the right side of the hall, wearing a black blazer and slacks. He walked confidently, with four bars embroidered on his sleeves. His hair was silver and cut short, and a briefcase was at his side. She would've missed him altogether if she hadn't looked up because he quickly disappeared down a corridor to the right. Reflexively, Julie followed him. She lagged behind to avoid being noticed, but stayed close enough to not lose sight of him. He rounded another corner and Julie trailed behind. It was busier in this part of the hospital, but the man was easy to spot. He passed through a set of doors under the sign that Julie had been looking for.

```
Intensive Care Unit
```

She hesitated. The whole thing felt surreal. Honestly, she couldn't even be sure if this pilot had anything to do with the accident. The door under the sign was unlocked, so this was her chance. It wasn't even about publishing; it was about something more. Things with Ryan had suddenly become uncertain, but here the step forward was hers alone to take. This strange story was only becoming more interesting and possibility was drawing her in. In a split-second decision, she passed through the doors just before they closed.

The ICU was different from the rest of the hospital. It was freshly renovated, with an open hallway and patient rooms on each side. As Julie cautiously passed through the doors, staff hustled around her. The ward was surrounded by glass from floor to ceiling, so the patients in beds and on ventilators were on display. She could see machines and wires attached to the afflicted, beneath veils of thin cloth. It was an unnerving sight, unlike anything she had seen before.

The uniformed pilot was five rooms away. He had slowed to a stop and was gazing through the glass on his right. For several moments, he watched with his hands hidden in his pockets. His shoulders were slumped. Even from a distance, she could see grief weighing on him. Finally, he turned away and vanished into a room behind him. Julie came close enough to see the sign on the door he disappeared behind.

```
ICU Waiting Room
```

Through a window, she saw him toss his blazer onto a chair and start pacing.

She then turned around and approached the glass he had been looking through. It was a hospital room lit only by the glow of a downward light. There was a young man swathed in a thin drape lying in a position that allowed her to see his face. His eyes were closed, and a clear tube was protruding from his mouth. Wires and tubes connected him to machines that buzzed and beeped. Though he looked young, his face was drained of color. His arms were propped on pillows and he looked weak. On each side, a man and woman were seated, one crying and the other stoic. The fragility of life had never felt so real to Julie.

A second passed before Julie realized they weren't alone. There was another person standing in the back of the room, beyond the lamp's ring of light. He was wearing an oversized grey sweatsuit, and his eyes were cast to the floor. But when Julie turned to leave, he looked up. In an instant, their eyes locked. The hair on her arms stood on end and her ears began to ring. She wanted to flee but was locked in his gaze.

In his eyes, there was neither grief nor sadness. There wasn't melancholy or sorrow. She felt like a trapped animal. She begged her feet to take a step, but they remained still. The man's jaw grew tight, and his fists balled. There was only one emotion she could recognize in his glare.

It was fury.

Chapter 11

September 2024 | Avionica Airlines Headquarters
Tampa Bay, Florida

High in the Avionica Tower, Michael slumped in his desk. His corner office was lush, with stunning views of the coast. There were dark mahogany bookcases filled with plaques and pictures, and a leather couch tucked in the corner. When he had started here, this had all been a tasty perk of the job. He had pictured himself commanding the company from here and bringing about record-breaking success. His post came with power and his appetite for it was vast. The power inspired fear, and he had ruled with a heavy hand. It was the reason for his success, and the way he had gotten here.

Michael had quickly learned the power came at a steep price.

In a few short months, this company had gutted him dry. In an attempt to salvage his marriage, he had signed the mortgage papers for a multi-million-dollar house. The purchase had been a plea for his wife to stay. Unfortunately, it had not been enough. It hadn't been enough for his first wife either. His career had cannibalized everything, and this marriage was yet another sacrifice. Of course, his problems with the bottle and a mean streak hadn't helped either. All he had left in this life was this company, and he couldn't lose it. Michael needed to preserve himself at any cost. They would have to claw this job out of his cold, dead hands.

He was alone in his office: the shades were drawn, and the lights were off. It was dark and the only noise was the tinkling of ice in his glass. It was hot outside, so he had chosen gin.

Today's board meeting had been unnerving but not unusual. Michael ran the business under a watchful, spiteful eye. Even from Luxton's beach home in Chile or mountain chateau in the Alps, Michael felt his presence. Every decision he made was being watched, and it kept him awake at night. Now, it would only be worse.

It was just after two in the afternoon, and he was thankful the gin was cutting into his angst. He knew he should not be drinking now because he couldn't afford any mistakes. He had to clean things up, Luxton had made that clear. He had days, not weeks. The situation had gotten out of control so quickly that it seemed almost impossible to fix. The news was buzzing around out there, and the FAA was circling. Things were bleak, that was certain, and he needed to act. Unfortunately, there were few options and none of them were good. Whatever the decision, he needed to prove his worth to Luxton.

Michael swung the last of the gin down his throat. The aromatic sting of juniper berries resonated in his sinuses.

There was a knock at the door. "Sir," a young woman said as she entered. She was tall and slim with a grey skirt cut above the knees. "Chief Pilot Jett Fitzgerald just called." She was uneasy, sensing his ire. "The co-pilot's family is visiting him in the hospital."

"Is Brewer there?" he asked, tossing the glass on his desk. He needed that captain to get out of there. He had been the senior pilot on that flight, so he needed him to stay the hell away. He knew too much. Of all the pilots to be involved in this mess, the fact it was Frank Brewer only made this situation worse. He was a stubborn, difficult son-of-a-bitch and would only make scrubbing this away harder.

"Both the chief and Captain Brewer are there." The woman stayed in the doorway as she spoke.

"You tell Jett Fitzgerald to stay there until I say otherwise," he said sharply. It seemed the chief pilot was his only tool for keeping this mess from getting worse. Fortunately, he was loyal; he had proven it many times before. Burben got to his feet and began to pace. How to proceed wasn't clear yet, but each passing second was making a decision more urgent. Thankfully, he had always been more creative after a few drinks. "You tell the chief to get Frank Brewer the hell out of there."

Without another word, the young woman exited through the oak doors and closed them quietly behind her.

Chapter 12

September 2024 | Hennepin County Medical Center
Minneapolis, Minnesota

"You've gotta be kidding me," Frank said between his teeth. He didn't hide his sudden anger when he saw the young woman peering through the glass in the ICU hallway. "They've got a lot of goddamn nerve!"

After everything that had happened that day, sending more corporate pawns here was salt in his wounds. Cameron, his young first officer, was ailing in bed while another company leech watched. She had probably volunteered to come, to make a name for herself so she could climb the company ladder. The thought made him sick. He wouldn't let this happen, not after today. Frank stormed out of the hospital room to confront her. She was not wearing the usual conservative company attire, but he could see right through that. She was speechless, visibly surprised, which only infuriated Frank.

"They already sent Jett," Frank said outside of the door. He knew the chief pilot had only been sent to put out fires. "We don't need more of you here to watch." Frank stood over the woman while his raised voice turned heads. He knew his temper was getting the better of him, but he was exhausted and had a right to be angry. Nine people were lying in this hospital, one of them critical.

They had trusted him to keep them safe. Of course, there is always some risk in flying, but this was something else entirely. What had happened could have been avoided. No matter what they said, Jett and this woman knew exactly why they were all here.

"You corporate bastards could've stopped this," he said. The woman flinched and her silence only fueled Frank's rage. "If you gave one single shit about safety rather than money," he was pointing at her now, "this never would've happened." For once in his career, he felt someone in the company was finally listening. She had nowhere to run to, so he wasn't going to miss his chance. "We *all* know these engines should've been fixed *years* ago," his mind was racing. The thought cut deep. Things had been hushed up at every level, he knew that, but the sting also cut close to home. For years, he had looked the other way too.

"This has happened too many times." A nurse was slowly approaching the scene. "We all know you manage to keep it silent, however the hell you do that." The woman remained perfectly still. "This Aerotoxic *bullshit* should've been worked out years ago!"

Just as the final syllable fell out of Frank's mouth, the door of the ICU waiting room opened. The uniformed pilot emerged.

"Who is this, Frank?" asked Jett. His hushed tone was at odds with Frank's demeanor. Calmly, he came into the hallway adjusting his slacks at the belt. Frank slowly began to feel people's eyes on him, including those from the pair beside Cameron's hospital bed.

Frank was stumbling over his own momentum. "What do you mean?" he scoffed. His skin was hot and his forehead damp. "This is one of yours, Jett," he pointed at the woman. He wasn't going to be deceived. "She's with the airline."

The chief pilot smiled diplomatically. He waved at the onlookers, as if to assure all was well, and opened the waiting room door. He gestured for Frank and the woman to file in.

"Now that we've made quite the scene," the chief eyed Frank before turning to Julie. "Who are you exactly?" He smiled at her politely.

"What are you talking about, Jett?" spat Frank. "Don't play games."

"I'm sorry to bother you..." The woman was clearly startled and struggling to get words out. Both men waited urgently. She hesitated and blushed. "I am Julie," she started. Her eyes darted between the two of them. "Professor Julie Sampers, from the University of North Dakota Aviation Department."

There was a silence. The chief looked at Frank, whose dazed eyes kept looking ahead. He was speechless.

"The University of North Dakota?" Jett finally asked. He rubbed his mustache.

"That's correct," she said, adjusting the bag over her shoulder.

"Who sent you?" Frank cut.

"No one sent me," she said. She shifted uncomfortably.

"Then why the hell are you here?" Frank's voice grew.

"Thank you very much for coming, Professor," said the chief pilot. He extended his hand coolly. "We are caring for our valued pilot," he gestured across the hall. He spoke evenly. "We are here to take care of him and his family in this terrible time." As if something had switched, the tone changed in an instant. "That's how we care for our team, you see." Frank looked over at the chief pilot, also surprised by the sudden flip. "What happened was a freak accident." He emphasized the words "freak" and "accident". "At Avionica Airlines, safety is our focus."

The pilot grinned. Julie was stunned.

"Now, if you'll excuse us," he opened the door and guided her by the shoulder. "I think it'd be best if we got back to taking care of our pilot." Jett smiled a final time, but Frank remained silent. Julie looked over her shoulder as she was lightly guided through the door. "Have a nice evening, Ms. Sampers."

Intrepid Pursuit

Chapter 13

September 2024 | Avionica Airlines Headquarters
Tampa Bay, Florida

Behind his desk, Michael stared across the Atlantic. It was nearing dusk and the sun was just falling behind the horizon. He tilted his head back, letting the last drops of gin fall down his throat.

The deep ocean hue followed the curve of the earth. The only way to see where the ocean stopped and the sky began was to look for the exact point where the color changed. During the day it was easy, obvious even: the wispy light of the sky was at odds with the sea. But at dusk, it wasn't so clear. The barrier between earth and sky merged. The gin was warm in his blood, and his previous hesitation was being displaced by resolve. His feet were up on his desk and his hands interlaced behind his head. He took in the scene, savoring the moment.

Far off, storm clouds were brewing. A grey haze of rain was falling towards the ocean beneath them. Below his office, the beaches were humming with tourists walking the twilight hours. Some caught a final dip for the evening while others enjoyed the last few minutes of sunset from the shore. There were hundreds, each in their own world, but Michael could see every one of them from his perch. Not a single one could hide. He knew something they didn't, and he relished the power. There was a storm coming and their time was limited.

It had been years since Michael had felt helplessness. Today, it had been holding him by the neck. He had felt powerless, but worse, he had been feeling reactive and vulnerable. It was a dreadful state but something he intended to forget. Things would change, that was certain, and the warm grit of gin reminded him that nothing could stop him. Perhaps it was the storm growing to the south. Maybe it was the assistant who fixed his drink or the chauffeur waiting for him outside. Whatever it was, the tides were changing. Tonight, he had remembered why he was at the helm of this multi-million-dollar company.

Michael could make people perform. Under any circumstance, they obeyed.

The phone rang. On his desk, he clicked the speakerphone.

"Yes." He spoke decisively, his voice like a blade. He came to his feet and leaned over his desk. It was Jett Fitzgerald.

"Sir," the chief pilot hesitated, "somebody came to the hospital."

"What are you talking about?" said Michael.

"There was a woman," said Jett, choosing his words carefully. "She was asking questions."

"Why are you wasting my time with this," fired the VP. He could hear uncertainty and he didn't have the patience for it. "It's your job to deal with this shit."

"Sir..." the chief continued. He cleared his throat, audibly uneasy. "Things are a little more complicated." Michael waited impatiently, looking at his empty glass.

"Get it out, Jett."

"She was told some information." Jett was on guard but spoke evenly. "It was thought that she was from the airline."

"You listen to me." Michael leaned over his desk on closed fists. "Clean this up, do you hear me?" The chief pilot muttered in agreement, but the executive wasn't listening. "I don't want to hear from you until you figure it out."

"Yes, sir," he said. "I will figure it out."

"I question what you can even handle," Michael said. His words were a little slippery now. He grabbed the empty glass, rolling it in his hand. He knew that there are two things people want in the world: money and power. In this company, the first was easy to come by. It was abundant if you played your cards right. But the latter was more complicated. People who want power can be idealistic and are more challenging to overcome. Moving money was easy, but there was only one way to curve a person seeking power. You must crush them.

"There will not be any more problems, sir."

"Who was it?" Michael asked, still rolling the glass in his hand. He looked back towards the Atlantic, seeing the storm grow nearer. To take stock of the enemy was the mark of a wise warrior. "The woman. Who was the woman?"

"She said her name was Julie Sampers," the chief pilot said. "A professor from the University of North Dakota."

But before Chief Pilot Jett Fitzgerald could say more, the line went dead.

Chapter 14

September 2024 | University of North Dakota
Grand Forks, North Dakota

The arena thrust into the sky, towering higher than any building in the south end of campus. Columns of red brick bordered vaulted panes of glass under the white dome that covered several city blocks. The building glowed with a warm hue that could be seen for miles across town. It was Saturday night, and the bite of fall was cutting through the air. There was no snow yet, but the crisp air said it was coming.

The city had been buzzing with anticipation. It was game day and, from the organic grocer to the trucking company near the highway, people had hustled through their work. Students across campus had made plans for where they'd be when the puck dropped. Even for those who never bothered with sports, hockey was a way of life here. It was Friday night and TVs in homes and bars across town were flipped to the local channel. The university band began a brassy tune in 4/4 time and cheerleading ice skaters sailed across the ice. Hundreds of people in white and green jerseys flooded the grand entrance of the Ralph Engelstad Arena for the first game of the season. Though North Dakota had no professional sports team, UND Men's Hockey seemed to fill the role and more.

William Hoffman

Inside the first-floor entrance, Professor Julie Sampers pulled the scarf from around her neck. Crowds headed towards their seats in the celebratory atmosphere. The arched ceiling rose six stories above her and hanging escalators shuttled fans between each concourse. The concession stands were busy, and a local cover band sang an old John Mellencamp tune. The beer flowed easily, and the sweet smell of roasted almonds warmed the air. The arena was said to be one of the finest in the country and its 12,000 leather seats made it among the largest. Ralph Engelstad's $104 million donation had funded the structure often called the "Taj Mahal" of hockey.

As much as she wished she wasn't, Julie was nervous. Navigating the busy concourse, she made her way to the elevators. The box seats were on the top floor and she anxiously headed there. She never did well at these sorts of things. The small talk was forced, and she would be counting down the minutes until she could escape. She was socially awkward, but more importantly, she found small talk exhausting. For much of her life, she had managed to avoid gatherings like this, but now things were different.

The young professor took a deep breath, trying again to calm her nerves. On the top floor, she stepped out of the elevator. Dutifully waiting, a suited waiter greeted her with cold, fizzing champagne. She accepted it and eyed the space. The room was dazzling, with rich cherry wood paneling and billiard-green carpeting. Suited faculty members were milling around, most holding a cocktail and a plate. A sign read *UND Department of Aerospace,* and the warm scent of buttery garlic swirled in the air among the chatter of colleagues. Behind a table, a woman greeted Julie while passing her a name tag.

Julie Sampers
Assistant Professor of Aerospace

She clipped it on her blouse, fighting a nervous tickle in her stomach. The last time she had been at an event this fancy had been at this very one a year ago. More than anything, she wanted to blend in. The room was full of familiar faces eating cocktail weenies and honeyed ham. Every surface seemed to be covered by either a tray of appetizers or bouquets of flowers. The clatter of ice in glass tinkled through the sound of conversation, which was increasingly raucous thanks to the open bar. At the far end of the box was a panoramic view of the ice below. The stands were packed with students and fans, waiting for the puck to drop.

It was an event the Department of Aerospace faculty conducted at the beginning of each academic year, in a reserved box on the top ring. The Ralph Engelstad Arena was one of the most sought-after venues in the city. Professors were chatting about research plans while others caught up after a summer's break. Julie stood near the entrance with her untouched glass of champagne. Looking around the room, certain things were clear. She was the youngest in the faculty and one of only a few women. But of all the things on her mind, it wasn't the differences that made her uneasy. She was used to being alone and having to fend for herself. It was something else, something more nuanced that was making her tense.

Julie was nervous because she understood why these events were so important.

This place, these people, held her future in their hands. After years of finding her way, it finally felt like she had found a place where she belonged. But despite her progress, her future was on the line now. If she played her cards incorrectly, she could lose it all. She was nervous because events like these mattered in academia. These connections were essential, and a simple conversation could decide her career. Julie swallowed heavily as a punchline brought a group by the bar to laughter. She spun the glass in her fingers, again surveying the room. As the hockey players began to circle on the ice below, she knew that these people would be the ones who would decide if she could stay.

But Julie had more on her mind. It wasn't just her job that had been keeping her awake for the previous few nights. Upon returning to the university, she had been distracted. She thought often about the man in the grey sweatsuit and the young pilot in the hospital bed. It was the rage in the man's eyes that she couldn't shake off, and she wondered about what had been unsaid. Her mind formed explanations both plausible and absurd. The man in the grey sweat suit had been angry, but it was more than that: he had been pleading. She sensed there was more to the story than whatever it was that she had stumbled upon in the ICU, but was uncertain how to take things further. She had been on edge, her mind constantly racing, so she had resorted to the only way she knew of to quell her nerves. When things were uncertain, Julie turned inward. Since she'd returned from Minneapolis, she had read endlessly. She had dove into the stack of articles from the library late into the night, consuming them page by page. Some she read once, but others many more times. All the while, she was stringing the story together piece by piece. She needed to arm herself with everything there was to know about Aerotoxic Syndrome.

The earliest papers had been published as far back as the 1950s. The text described mysterious symptoms after an unknown chemical filled an airplane. The haze enclosed unknowing passengers and began to take its insidious toll. As Ron had said, the reports had only come from airliners powered by jet engines, which had been new to the industry at the time. With each report, the symptoms began to emerge in greater detail. After the fog appeared, there was dizziness and blurry vision. Then came painful fits of coughing and gasping. Within minutes, some people would completely faint. Year after year, there were more papers and the evidence piled up. The syndrome seemed to follow a similar pattern but always packed the same blow. Early papers gave it many names like *Aircraft Toxic Syndrome* or *Flying Sickness,* but a paper published in 1990 coined the name that seemed to stick: Aerotoxic Syndrome. The leading culprit was a chemical called tricresyl phosphate. TCP, a synthetic oil used as a jet engine lubricant, appeared to be at the center of the problem. An organophosphate toxic to humans, the chemical seemed to come up in every paper she read. But if it was as serious as it seemed, she couldn't understand why it was so unfamiliar. It felt impossible that she had never heard of this all before. She dug into the details, taking meticulous notes. Amid the minutiae, one thing stood out. After reading every paper she could get her hands on, it all came back to one thing. The mystery was not so mysterious. Every paper ultimately pointed to the same smoking gun.

The hydraulic seal near the engine drive pump.

When the seal became leaky, pressurized air forced the lubricant, ripe with TCP, right into the cabin. Sometimes there would be an odor, other times there was no clue, but each time the chemical leaked, it would wreak havoc. Unsuspecting passengers and crew would fall ill, and the airliner was in danger. Across all the episodes, there was a pattern: the type of airplane, the symptoms, and the scene. There would be coughing and wheezing, along with vague, neurological symptoms. A paper would be published in the scientific literature with a warning cry, but nothing would follow. Once the urgency of the situation subsided, the panic would clear. There were no major newspaper articles, no news segments and no outcry. Word of the events would pop up here and there, but it would eventually fade and Julie could not figure out why. Smoky cabins and sick passengers were certainly newsworthy, so something about it did not add up.

"Welcome back, professor!" said Professor Rover, pulling Julie from her thoughts. "I'm glad to see you made it."

Julie turned, relieved to see a familiar face. "I sure am happy to see you, Ron," she said. Near the door, they stood overlooking the party. Ron had been attending this event for decades, but he had arrived without pomp and circumstance.

"So," he smiled, "How did things go in Minneapolis?" A bow-tied waiter passed, and Ron helped himself to a glass of red wine.

"Strange," she started. She was relieved Ron was here, not knowing who else she could bring herself to chat with. "Honestly, I don't know what to make of it."

"It's a curious thing," said Ron. He grabbed a treat off another passing tray. "There's been whispers about this sort of thing for years."

"I think I found the pilot," she said. In the arena below, the players circled on the ice. "They said a lot," her mind replayed the night. *"We all know these engines should've been fixed years ago..."* The announcer began listing names, each followed by gleeful applause. "They thought I was from the airline." Ron raised his eyebrows, curious but not enough to miss another passing tray of vol-au-vents. She told him about how the man in the grey sweatsuit had described the problems with engines. "They said something about the engines," Julie almost whispered. "He was furious." Ron simply watched as he gulped down the last of his wine.

"Did you tell them who you were?" he asked.

"There was another man there," she said. Julie looked at her glass. "I think he was a senior pilot," she looked up. "Maybe even their chief." There was another tray of full wine glasses and Ron helped himself. "That's when they realized I wasn't from the airline." Her forefinger picked at her thumbnail. "I told them the truth."

"Does the name Oliver Jaxon ring a bell?" he asked. He took a sip while Julie thought. The name was a vaguely familiar name, but Julie couldn't immediately place it.

"Professor Jaxon is an impressive man." Ron scratched his nose and waved politely at another passing faculty member. "He must be in his 60s by now, but he's done a great deal of publishing on the subject. In fact, he made a name for himself based on his research on Aerotoxic Syndrome in the 1980s." Julie realized she had seen the name in the stack of papers she had been reading. "After the FAA discredited it all, Jaxon seemed to fall from high and his work was largely forgotten. The odd thing is that I haven't seen anyone else take on the issue."

Julie had read the news release published by the government in the fall of 2000. Once and for all, the FAA had tried to put the issue to rest. They had refuted Aerotoxic Syndrome and said there was no reason for people to worry. They had encouraged people to travel with confidence, claiming that the US aviation system was among the safest in the world. But as Julie delved into the history, she couldn't help but wonder if their conclusions had been based on quality science or on economics. Certainly, thousands of faulty airplanes didn't bode well for a multi-billion-dollar aircraft manufacturer that paid hefty taxes for sales to US carriers. She had also noticed that not a single new paper had been published on the topic for nearly 25 years.

A new crop of faculty members filled the room and additional trays of plated appetizers were dispatched. The glug of pouring wine sung among trumpets touting the university hymn.

"Why don't you reach out to his office and see if you can talk to him?" Ron suggested. The call and response of the university fight-song began. "I'm not sure there is a better expert in the world."

The need to publish had been weighing on Julie for so long. She walked the halls with dread, worrying the Dean would pull her into his office. There were easier projects she could have undertaken, but she was being pulled to this story. She had been lying awake at night thinking about the young pilot in the ICU and where things had gone wrong. Not only did she need to publish, but something about this also felt personal. Perhaps her strengths didn't include the nuances of academic life, but something else about this fit neatly into her wheelhouse. There was more to this story and Julie wanted to find it.

At that moment, the first puck of the season dropped. The massive UND forward swiped it from his opponent and skated around two advancing defensive men. Only 20 feet from the center of the ice, the UND forward pulled his stick back and eyed the goal. Spectators held their breath collectively as their player took a bold and decisive slapshot, barreling the puck down the center of the ice. The puck accelerated towards the slot and fans came to their feet. The goalie jolted into a defensive position, but it was no use. As it passed through his legs and into the net, the stadium erupted.

Chapter 15

September 2024 | University of North Dakota
Grand Forks, North Dakota

The UND *Fighting Hawks* Men's Hockey team had won their first game of the season, generating momentum many hoped would carry them through the long winter ahead. Outside the stadium gates, gleeful fans cheered and laughed. There was music and a growing sea of jerseys filling the sidewalks. A group of sorority sisters were arm and arm and smiling for the camera, while rows of buses were ready to drive fans to bars. Some students walked towards the dorms while others headed to their trucks and homes. Grand Forks saw traffic jams infrequently, but just after ten o'clock on Saturday evening in the hockey season was one of the few times it did.

Julie distractedly stepped out into the evening air. A student's voice called the University cry from behind her, "Sioux yea yea!" and everyone around called back cheerfully: "Yea Sioux Sioux!" There was laughing and clapping, but Julie tuned it out. She could only think about what lay ahead of her. The stadium lights faded and the crowd thinned as she got further from campus and closer to home.

Intrepid Pursuit

At a function like tonight, Julie should've been elbowing her way to the department chair. She should have attempted small talk, tried to make him laugh, and most importantly she should have aimed to show him she was here and intended to stay. Knowing and acting are two different things though, and she had done none of it. Instead, she had stayed put, hugging the back wall with her glass of champagne. She had spent the evening going over everything that had happened in Minneapolis. In many ways she was galvanized, and certainly she was curious, but she also felt something else. In considering it all, Julie felt a little uneasy. It was hard to rationalize it all. Could it really be negligence? She trusted the system and it seemed to work, evidenced of millions of safe passengers every year. But to think there was something malicious going on that could impact people's lives struck a chord with Julie. If people were truly turning away from this, there would be no way that she could too.

Back in her apartment, she tossed her keys on her desk. Sitting by her dish, Amelia called out for dinner. Julie filled the bowl, then paged through the stack of articles on her table again. Like a deck of cards, she shuffled through them hoping for some luck. Ron was right, Professor Oliver Jaxon was the author of most of them. Some articles described the biochemistry of TCP while others discussed the economics of Aerotoxic Syndrome. Some were less than a page long while some were exhaustive. It was clear why he had been the premiere name when it came to Aerotoxic Syndrome. Oliver Jaxon was among the most prolific aerospace researchers she had ever encountered.

In the coming days, Julie had a single focus: to speak to Oliver Jaxon. Her work was otherwise put on hold while she tried to connect with him day and night. Google told her he was a professor at King's College in London and a recreational pilot. It didn't take much digging to discover pictures of his sporty yellow biplane. The university website had his contact information, but her countless calls and emails were left unanswered. With London six hours ahead of North Dakota, Julie tried at all hours of the day. To catch someone in the morning, she called late at night. Later, she tried in the early morning to catch someone over the English lunch hour. Days came and went without success. Progress was elusive and the odds of speaking with him seemed to be getting increasingly bleak. After a week, it was clear she needed a new plan. The passing of time weighed down on her and she felt she needed to make at least some progress. But it was an idea that came to her one Saturday morning that made a new path forward clear.

William Hoffman

The bottom of the sun was still below the horizon and the birds were calling their morning song. Changing leaves blew easily in the autumn air. She was on a jog, a favorite part of her daily routine, and she cut out of downtown towards the river. The Green Way Trail connected eight miles along the Red River Basin and Julie knew it like it was her own backyard. Since freshman year, she had been using these trails to escape and think. She never ran to music because her best ideas always came on the trail.

At the north end, a bridge connected both sides of the Red River. She stopped at the center, looking north toward Lake Winnipeg. Her breath was heavy, and she leaned on the railing. Above her, wisps of cirrus clouds were painted high in the stratosphere. Higher than any aircraft would fly, the nuanced lines cut across the sky. At the center, an airliner was flying west. The temperature was far below zero at that altitude and contrails were tracking from the wings. Julie studied it for a moment, still amazed that hundreds of people could be suspended in such a small point in space. It was a feat of human ingenuity and Julie appreciated it for what it was: a miracle.

It was then that it occurred to her.

Julie could not solve this alone. She had the drive and some of the tools, but she needed more. What Julie needed was information. Professor Oliver Jaxon, the world's expert, was elusive and the airline would not talk. The problem was pressing, but for some reason Julie was possibly the only one listening. Standing on the bridge looking skyward, Julie realized she had another option. The professor and the airline were not the only sources of information. Onboard that plane in Minneapolis had been hundreds of witnesses. Turning back towards home, she ran faster. Her breathing was heavy, but she did not slow.

"Hello?" After the toneless ring of the phone, a baritone voice came on the line. It was late in the evening, the sun long having set.

"Is this Mr. Mauricio?" Julie inched forward on the couch, pressing the phone to her ear. After a week of dead ends, this felt like a rush forward. "This is Julie Sampers."

Intrepid Pursuit

"Yes, this is Philip," said the man. A Latin melody played in the background. "I was surprised to hear from you."

"I am interested to know what happened to you," she said urgently. She was trying to stay cool, but she was out of her comfort zone. She was a professor, not a reporter, and she felt keenly aware of her inexperience. "I appreciate you responding to my message."

The idea was simple. From the newspaper article, Julie knew the name of a man who had been on that flight. He had been quoted saying that there had been smoke, and she had circled his name. It was him that she needed to speak with.

"Listen, I'm not sure I can help you," he cut in. The tune in the background concluded and was quickly followed by another. "There's not much to say."

The newspaper article had only included two pieces of information: his name and the fact that he lived in Miami. Tracking him down hadn't been an easy feat, but Julie was diligent. Starting at the top, she had sent a Facebook message to every Philip Mauricio she could find in Miami. She had sent hundreds of messages asking for connections with flight 1846. Some replied, most of them obviously gags, but she had finally stumbled upon one that seemed legit. It hadn't been highly nuanced detective work, but the ends seemed to justify the means.

"Well," Julie hesitated. She wished she had spent more time preparing her questions. She struggled to clearly state the thoughts that were spinning in her mind. "Any information would be helpful."

"Avionica said the pilot was sick and they had to land." She could sense an uneasiness in his voice. She stood up and paced in front of her couch. "It is as simple as that."

"You told the newspaper there was smoke in the cabin," she said. She wished her pulse would stop rushing in her ears. She was a pilot and had been trained to keep her nerves cool, but the adrenaline was getting the best of her. The man was silent, and Julie hoped she hadn't already blown it.

"I'm not sure what you're talking about, Ms. Sampers," said the man. He sounded more guarded now. "I must've been mistaken."

"You're saying the smoke you told reporters about didn't happen?" she asked. It was a curveball she hadn't been expecting.

"I'm not sure what I saw," he said. His words were faster now, his tone anxious. Julie was worried he was going to hang up. She sensed the clock was ticking but she needed to keep him on the phone. He was her only lead and she needed to wring him like a sponge.

"Let's start here," she made her voice quieter, trying to recover. "Where were you traveling that day, sir?"

The only sound that came through the phone was a syncopated beat of the song's refrain. Julie could almost hear the man thinking but she knew he had the next move. Why was he so defensive? He wasn't acting like the victim of an aviation accident. Julie couldn't explain it. Unless, of course, there was something else.

"Look," he started. "What happened that day is behind us. The airline told me they would make sure it didn't happen again." He cleared his throat. "I haven't thought about it since."

"Make sure what didn't happen again?" Julie followed. Her mind was racing. He didn't want to talk, that was clear. But what she didn't understand was why this man would bother calling back if he didn't have something to say.

"Like I said," he struggled. "I'm not sure exactly what happened." Time seemed to slow. "Now, if you'll excuse me, I'm working on some things and…"

"Look, Mr. Mauricio," Julie interrupted. This was it, her last chance. "I know something happened on that airplane. There's something you're not telling me." She was desperate and held her breath. Taking a leap, she could lose it all. "I'm asking for your help," she begged. The man was silent. The only reason she knew he had not hung up was that she could still hear the muffled waltz through the phone. "Help me make sure this really never happens again."

Intrepid Pursuit

Julie's eyes were fixed forward, focused past her window on the city beyond. It was a clear night, with no clouds to block the stars. She pressed her phone harder to her ear, hoping for more. All the while, Philip said nothing. She begged him silently, hoping for anything. She was waiting for the universe to signal that she was doing the right thing.

But instead, there was an exhale and then a click. In the silence, Julie's eyes widened. With the dial tone, her eyes closed in defeat.

Chapter 16

September 2024 | Downtown
Grand Forks, North Dakota

Julie held her eyes shut for several long seconds. When they opened, she prayed for different circumstances. A subtle headache squeezed at her temples and she suddenly realized how tired she was. She hadn't eaten anything all day and her mouth was dry. Despite a tiresome week, she had nothing to show for it. It was after midnight and the weight of defeat was beginning to press. Long hours of research had brought the history together, but she still could not connect the flight in Minneapolis to Aerotoxic Syndrome with any certainty. She had reason to believe a problem many decades in the making had put those people in the hospital, but she still had nothing to go on. Honestly, she was beginning to wonder if she was just wasting her time. Not only had her leads turned up dry, but she had put every other part of her job on hold. She didn't even want to think about her email inbox and everything else that she had ignored this week. It would be impossible to catch up. Perhaps Aerotoxic Syndrome was still hurting people, but it seemed the world had forgotten about it. Maybe there was a reason why.

Intrepid Pursuit

On the coffee table, her computer was open. There was a news article with the title running across her screen. She exhaled, feeling the text only affirmed what worried her. The article came out this afternoon. She tried to look past it, hoping it was a mistake, but now she was beginning to reconsider. It all seemed to fit: the smoke, the pilot in the hospital, and the man in the grey sweats in Minneapolis. She had thought it through countless times and the history and science seemed to all point towards Aerotoxic Syndrome. But now, after speaking to Philip Mauricio, she wondered if she was chasing smoke. A news outlet in Minneapolis had run the story and she skimmed the text again.

```
NTSB preliminary report: Avionica incident resulted
from pilot medical emergency, does not suspect
equipment failure or error.
```

Maybe it was all nothing.

Perhaps all this lost sleep had been over something that had a simpler explanation. Investigators were likely doing their due diligence and it was possible the co-pilot had simply fallen ill. The man in the grey sweat suit could easily be a disgruntled employee and maybe Aerotoxic Syndrome really was debunked. It was hard to argue for much else at the moment.

Amelia jumped onto the couch and flicked her tail. She purred when Julie scratched the right spot, and then settled in a corner when she was satisfied.

Then the phone rang.

It was unexpected, and Julie hesitated before leaning forward. For several long seconds, she didn't answer it.

Buzz.

She studied the screen, and her heart began to beat faster. It was an unsaved number but one she recognized in an instant. *Miami, Florida.* She got to her feet.

"Hello?" she said.

"It's me," said the man. His words were curt. She recognized his voice but noticed the background music had ceased. "I had to step out," he said. There was an air of caution in his voice.

"Philip?" Julie said, trying to regain her bearings. She did not know where to start.

"I shouldn't say anything," he started. He paused, as if looking over his shoulder. "They told me not to."

"*Who* told you?" Julie asked.

"Who do you think?" he asked. Julie stood perfectly still, waiting.

"After the accident, they called me," Philip continued. "They told me to stay quiet."

"About the smoke?" she asked.

"Yes," he cut her off, "about everything." She sensed their time was limited. Every second had to count. "No more newspapers," he said. "They told me not to even talk about it with my family."

"What else did they say?" She began to pick at her nail again. It was surreal and Julie wondered for a moment if it was a dream.

The man spoke quickly but quieter now. "They told me if I keep quiet," there was a hesitation, a calculating pause. "They'd pay me eight grand." Julie froze. Any hesitation that had been lurking moments before had vanished. "They said they were going to fix the problem." She could hear the uncertain satisfaction in his voice. It took her a second to realize what he was really saying. "They said they'd pay me to not talk about it anymore."

"What about the other passengers?"

"I didn't ask," he answered. She could feel the clock ticking. "The money came and I did what I was told."

Intrepid Pursuit

"What are they hiding?" Julie was losing him, she had to think quickly.

"I need to go," he said. Julie could hear new voices in the background, and he spoke almost in a whisper. "I can't say anymore."

"Wait, Mr. Mauricio," Julie stood on her toes. "Please!" There was so much more she needed to know.

"Don't say anything about the money," he said. "I really need it."

"Sir, if I can just ask you one more question…" she begged.

"Something happened on that plane though." He was no longer listening. "Something serious."

"Sir, please, if I can just ask you…" but the voices in the background grew louder.

"Delete this number and don't call me back."

"Philip, wait!"

The line went silent.

Chapter 17

September 2024 | Avionica Airlines Headquarters
Tampa Bay, Florida

The clock struck nine in the morning and Michael Burben was already aching for a drink. The sting of last night's gin was still stabbing deep behind his eyes, but it was a feeling he had grown accustomed to. It was how most of his days had begun recently.

Over a week had passed since this had all started, and the pressure was growing. He used the gin to deal with his nerves, but it was the hangovers that sustained the cycle. The fear of another unannounced visit from his boss was keeping him on edge. Employees were uneasy, and people were asking questions. The members of the board had been silent, but Michael knew there must be private talks. The company had been inundated with emails and phone calls after it all hit the news and it was a challenge to keep pace. Swathes of employees were working extra hours to meet the demand, causing overtime and rising expenses. This whole thing had already been expensive, but it was getting worse. People were nervous about the company and they had good reason to be. It was troubling to say the least, but Michael's lips were sealed. His job was to move this company forward and not to dwell on the past. He knew Bruce Luxton wouldn't tolerate much else.

The weekly reports were sitting on his desk. Luxton would be watching passenger numbers and revenue closely and Michael had been uneasy. If they were low, his future would be bleak. So much depended on these reports that it was hard to think of much else. Thankfully, the numbers weren't as bad as he had anticipated. In fact, they were pretty good. Flights were full and many were oversold. Revenue was surprisingly healthy, and cash-flow was strong. Capitalism was a beautiful thing: a simple aviation incident didn't seem to keep people from craving their cheap airline tickets.

Out of everything that happened the past week, there was one hand that had certainly been dealt in their favor. The preliminary National Transportation Safety Board investigation about the flight in Minneapolis had been good news. The document said an ill pilot had been to blame. They reported no mechanical failure or error, exactly like he had asked. In fact, the report suggested that the whole thing had been completely out of the airline's control. He had to smile. So much about the past week had made him question himself, but when his back was against the wall, he savored knowing that he could get results. He had learned early in his career it was helpful to have friends in high places, but experience had taught him an even more important lesson. If you don't have friends in high places, it is helpful to know that people in high places usually want money.

Michael pulled back the sleeve of his blazer and studied the hands of his Rolex GTM-Master II watch. It was quarter after nine. Time for that gin.

"Mr. Burben?" There was a knock at his office door. Through the mahogany frame, his secretary appeared. "You should probably see this." She was tall and thin, with breasts that pressed against her thin cotton shirt. He didn't want to admit how long it had been since he had felt the touch of a woman. He craved it. It was why he had given her the job. She closed the door and came forward. Michael remained impassive, watching her hips and trying to picture what was beneath her clothes.

"What is this?" he asked. She offered the piece of paper, but he didn't take it.

"This is an email we received," she said. "Requesting a comment about the incident in Minneapolis."

Michael grabbed the paper bitterly, grunting after the words. "There was no damn incident in Minneapolis." He skimmed it for no more than a second before throwing it back. "Who cares, we've gotten dozens of these."

The secretary didn't react. "I bring it to your attention because of the sender." She had become accustomed to his behavior.

"Unless it's from the owner of this company, I don't give a damn," he shot back.

"It's from a woman named Julie Sampers," she said. She stood unmoved before his desk. "From North Dakota."

It took him a second to place the name. "Christ," he mumbled under his breath. He took the paper again and read it closer.

"She wants to talk," said the woman. "We sent the formatted response, but she responded again." Michael looked up. "She is requesting details."

Michael's temperature was rising. He mumbled again and his ears were hot. Who the hell was this person? Since he had been a kid, he had always had a temper. Years of training had helped him get a grip on his rage, but moments like these put him to the test. He crumpled up the paper and threw it on his desk.

"Something needs to be done about this goddamn woman." Michael said. He spun his chair towards the window, where the wind was painting caps on the ocean waves. After her surprise visit to the hospital, he had figured he would never hear of her again. Apparently, things weren't going to be so simple. This could become an issue and she needed to be dealt with. Fortunately, he had the right skill set for this type of problem.

"I'll handle her myself."

Chapter 18

September 2024 | Carrollwood, Florida

The afternoon sun was beginning its oppressive push on the day and the air was heavy with moisture. The suburban Tampa neighborhood was quiet this time of day, with rows of ramblers left empty and locked for the afternoon. People were at work or engaged in retirement pastimes around town. The street was picturesque, with uniform homes on both sides and mailboxes set along the curb. Sprinklers clicked and a dog barked. A bald retiree pushed a lawnmower and palm trees were swaying in the hot breeze. In the driveway of his single-story home, Captain Frank Brewer stood with his phone pressed to his ear. He had just finished tending to his rows of summer lilacs and Egyptian star-clusters when it had rung in his pocket.

While aviation had been his life's work, Frank Brewer filled his days off the road tending to his garden. His job was stressful, but he found some stability in caring for his crop. It was an outlet, an escape from the pressure of the work, one that he depended on. But after a full week of long afternoons in his yard, he was on edge. The flight in Minneapolis had been over a week earlier but he still thought about it constantly. He had not flown since the emergency landing. In fact, he hadn't done much of anything since he had come home from the hospital. The airline had quietly given him paid time off, which he had cautiously accepted. But he wasn't naïve. They wanted him to keep a low profile and they were paying for it.

"Yes?" said Frank evenly into the line. He knew who was on the other end, but he wanted to make him say it.

"Hi Frank," said Chief Pilot Jett Fitzgerald. His words were friendly but forced. It was clear the chief was uneasy, but Frank didn't plan to give an inch. "I hope I didn't catch you at a bad time." Frank had been anticipating this call, but it wasn't one he had been looking forward to. The two pilots had been friends years before, but Frank's choice to stay in the cockpit and Jett's promotion up the corporate ladder had caused their friendship to wane. That had been a long time ago, and now they spoke only when necessary.

"Fine," Frank said. He caught some shade under his car port. He was on his guard and wasn't going to be fooled by pleasantries. "What can I help you with, Jett?"

"Well," Jett cleared his throat. The chief wasn't accustomed to being in such a defensive position. "I was just calling to check on you." He laughed nervously. "I wanted to see how you were doing."

"You're calling because they want me to start flying again." Frank hardly let him finish. He wasn't new at this; he understood how this airline worked. He saw no sense in bullshit. "They're losing money with a pilot out for so long."

"Only when you're ready, Frank," Jett sputtered. "We want you back when you're ready."

"What has been done to fix the problem, Jett?" Frank squinted, not interested in anything but the truth. He watched a silver-haired driver carting a Cadillac slowly down the street.

"It has been handled," the chief pilot said. His voice was sharper. "I'm handling it, Frank."

"I see you've managed to avoid a proper investigation," said Frank. "Again." Frank had seen the news article the day it came out. He had been incensed but not surprised. It was unbelievable to him that the federal government could let this go on. "I honestly don't know how you do it." He could only assume there was someone in D.C. with an interest in the airline's success because he knew what had really happened that day.

"Things are being handled, Frank." Jett's voice was harsher now, his patience evidently being stretched. Frank had touched a nerve. "You do your job and I'll do mine."

"You're kidding yourself if you think I'm getting back in the cockpit before something meaningful is done." Frank was becoming impatient too. "I won't stand by any longer. You and I both know what happened to Cameron," he said. Frank's co-pilot had been weighing on his mind since he'd returned from Minnesota. The guilt was crushing and getting stronger each day. While Frank was tending to his garden, the young pilot was in a rehab center trying to rebuild the person he had once been. It was a bitter truth, but he wasn't solely to blame. "This can't keep happening."

"Frank," he could hear the pain in his old friend's voice. "You need to be careful." The concern was the first genuine emotion Frank had heard. "You know how this company works and...." but his voice trailed. "Please, Frank."

"I don't give a damn about this company!" Frank fired back. His voice came out louder than he had intended. Under the awning of his garage, the captain pointed as he spoke. He was angry, but he knew it wasn't just about the company. He had known what was going on and he had stood by as a passive observer for years. In fact, they had all stood by. He knew others understood what was going on, but no one acted because they knew what would happen. However, this time the damage had happened on his watch. It was a bitter truth he would have to live with forever. But this week, he had made a promise to himself. Too many people had gotten in his way before, but he wouldn't stand for it any longer. He wouldn't be a cog in a wheel that turned profits at the expense of lives. Compared to other airlines, his pay was exceptional and his benefits generous, but it came at a cost. The money didn't seem to matter when he thought about the people that had paid for it, the people for whom he had been responsible. "We have a duty, Jett. I will *not* go back into the fleet until something is done about this."

"I was worried you would say that," said Jett. His tone changed. The pleading in his voice was gone, replaced quickly by remorseless momentum. "I'm authorized to give you another paid month of vacation and a thirty-five percent raise, Frank," he said. It was robotic, like the emotion was filleted out. "I can try to get more if you want."

The words stung Frank to his core. They were trying to buy him off, and the assault made him flinch. Before, he might have acceded, but not anymore. He had taken the money in the past, he had turned the other way, and now he was paying for it. He would not be that man any longer.

"Jett," his words were red-hot and slow. "I don't want your *fucking* money."

"Frank, please," Jett started. "Let's try and work something out."

"I will do *nothing* until this is fixed," Frank was unwavering. "And I hope you'd be man enough to do the same." There was a pause and Jett cleared his throat. Then there was the sound of shuffling papers and Frank held his breath.

"Well then Frank," said the chief pilot coldly, "you are fired. Effective immediately."

"What?!" Frank shot out the word. The shock knocked him breathless.

"We will destroy your credibility, Frank." The chief was stoic. He was detached, but not absent. "We will blame you for this." Frank's vision narrowed and his mouth hung open. "And if you come after us, we will fight you with everything we have."

"You're a coward!" Frank said through his teeth. The fog was clearing, allowing his fury to build. He should have seen this coming.

"I'll send someone to pick up your uniforms this afternoon," said Jett. "They will drop off your final paperwork."

"You're a goddamn sell out!" Frank yelled into the phone.

"Goodbye, Frank," said Jett, and then the line went silent.

Chapter 19

September 2024 | University of North Dakota
Grand Forks, North Dakota

"Knock knock!" said a familiar voice from the door. Julie looked up from her desk and smiled.

"Come in, Ron. Have a seat," she said. She stood and moved a stack of papers from the only other chair in her cramped office.

"I see you're hard at work," he said, looking at her desk. Julie sat back and studied the heap. Exam papers stared scornfully back at her. She didn't believe in multiple choice exams, knowing flying an airplane is anything but a multi-choice task, but it was tough not to regret it when it came time to grade essays.

"Getting through these slowly," she said. It usually took her several hours to correct every student's exam. It was meticulous but important work. However, she was distracted, and the task seemed unending. For many reasons, she had hardly slept. The sleep that had come had been restless and brief.

Since the phone call with Phillip, Julie had been at a crossroads. Her mind repeatedly dissected the evidence, trying to piece it all together. She thought about Dr. Jaxon and his decades of research that had come to such a sudden, mysterious halt. Below the surface, she sensed these were pieces of the same puzzle, but she couldn't fit them together. She felt no closer to the answer than when she had started.

At least that had been the case until a few hours earlier.

"Something happened this morning, Ron," she said. Remembering it sparked light in her.

"Is that so?" he turned curiously. She had never known him to get excited, and now he faced her with the simple openness he did with most things in life.

"I received an email early this morning," she said. Even sitting there now, Julie could hardly believe it. She set her pen on the stack and turned towards him. In a matter of a few hours, everything had changed. The past few weeks of anxious work finally meant something because she had been handed another piece to this story. "From the Englisg," Julie smiled. At the end of the dead end, she had discovered a trap door. "Oliver Jaxon's secretary sent me an email."

Rover rested his chin on his fist. The old man was surprised by few things, but she seemed to have his attention.

"I couldn't believe it," she continued. "I was beginning to think the whole thing would go nowhere."

"What did they say, Julie?" he asked curiously.

"It makes sense," she started. She picked at the nail of her index finger with her thumb. "I understand why they took so long to get back to me." In fact, she regretted trying so many times now. When they hadn't responded, Julie had been relentless. The unanswered calls and emails had piled up, and now she was a little embarrassed. "He wants me to come to London," she said. When the message had come, she had needed to read it twice to make sure she had really understood. "Jaxon is asking me to come right away."

Ron said nothing for a moment, letting the news nest in his mind. "He wants you to go to London to discuss the research?" he asked. He stroked the redundant skin on his cheeks.

"He wants to give me everything he has," she said. She could hardly believe it herself. "The data, his sources, his articles," she shook her head. "Everything!"

"Well, then." Ron straightened in his chair, his mind still catching up. Julie began tooling her nail with her front teeth. "You have to go." He smiled.

"They want me to come tomorrow morning," she said. "They said I have to come right away if I'm going to make the trip." For the entire morning, Julie had been wrapping her mind around it. It all felt so sudden, almost crazy, but she couldn't ignore tickle of excitement humming within her. The situation wasn't simple, and she understood why time was of the essence. "There's a reason he needs me to come so soon," she said. Julie looked at him closely, gauging his reaction. "Jaxon is dying," she said. "He's at home on hospice care." She waited. "His secretary thinks he only has a few days."

Ron was silent. He sat unmoved, his gaze far beyond the walls of her tiny office. Julie saw a man established in his field, well respected by his peers, guiding her in her path. In the field of aviation researchers, Professor Rover was among the elite. Julie had always wondered why he'd taken an interest in her, but in this moment she felt grateful.

"I'm just worried, Ron," she continued. She looked back on the stack of exams on her desk. "I have my lectures and I'm already so behind in everything else..."

"If he'll see you," Ron interrupted. "You must go."

"This project has been taking up so much of my time and everything else is falling through the cracks. I have my academic review in a few months, and I'm worried about the student feedback..."

"The world expert on Aerotoxic Syndrome is on his deathbed and he wants to speak to you," he said. He wasn't excited, but his eyes said everything. "This could be your shot, Julie," he said. Ron sat forward and tapped his hand on the desk. "I'll cover your lectures."

When Ron left, Julie was alone with her thoughts. She was buzzing with excitement, feeling the stir of a new adventure beginning. To think this project was hours from bringing her across the Atlantic seemed unbelievable, but she had to do it. Maybe after everything that had happened in the past few weeks, this was a signal to press forward. But unfortunately, there was more than just this project on her mind. Something else was also distracting her. The note from Jaxon wasn't the only message that she had received that morning. In fact, the second one had been nearly as unexpected as the first. While the first provoked excitement, the second took something from her. Alone in her office, Julie thought about it all again. In an instant, she felt small and vulnerable. It was a stinging reminder about who she could trust. The worst part was that she knew she had let it happen to herself.

Hours before boarding a plane to travel across the Atlantic, she was thinking again about Ryan.

She pulled out her phone and reread the message. It was at the top of her inbox.

RYAN RIFE @ 0814: There is someone else. I thought you understood what this was.

Chapter 20

September 2024 | Atlantic Ocean

Flying east towards England, Julie sat in the window seat of the airliner with a stack of articles and a cup of coffee. If she was to meet the world's expert in Aerotoxic Syndrome, everything he had ever published would have to be read and reread. With the ocean to her left, and an empty seat on her right, she spread out seven decades of research. Rereading it all would be no small task, but after another sip of coffee, she grabbed the next paper and started at the top.

Somewhere over the North Atlantic, she wrapped her head around the science. Stumbling over new words, she scribbled notes on what she'd need to look up later. She learned the details of how the neuron is the brain's way of sending signals around the body. Jaxon had described how toxic TCP, the leading suspect in Aerotoxic Syndrome, worked in the spaces between these neurons. Messages between neurons are sent by small amounts of chemicals called neurotransmitters. She read deliberately, her finger tracking along each sentence, but it slowly came together. She was a pilot, not a biologist, but Jaxon's writing was concise and intuitive. When a cabin full of unsuspecting passengers was filled with TCP, toxic quantities of neurotransmitters were released in their brains. The exposure propagated chaos and, in an airplane thousands of feet in the air, passengers had no way to escape. Symptoms were varied, from dizziness and blurry vision to headaches and seizures. Some coughed while others had swelling in their throats. Interestingly, some people experienced nearly nothing at all. It was a person's genetics, Jaxon had written, that accounted for why different people had varying degrees of symptoms. As strange as it was, some people seemed to metabolize the toxin faster than others. However it manifested, one thing was clear: TCP was a poison, wreaking life-changing damage on its victims.

The stewardess came by, and Julie accepted more coffee. It was late into the night in North Dakota, but the time changes made it difficult to keep track. As she worked through the stack, time didn't seem to matter. She knew she should rest, but the reading held her attention. Jaxon wrote with a passion that made the problem not only real, but personal. It seemed strange that so little had been done after decades of this problem, but Julie soon realized the explanation wasn't so mysterious.

It was an article published in 1998 that made it clear.

Jaxon had chronicled the curious story of a widebody airliner's overnight flight from San Francisco to Anchorage in 1974. Richard Nixon had just resigned, and Gerald Ford was the new president. It had been an unseasonably cool September when the routine flight had left California heading north. In fact, there had been nothing remarkable about the trip until, two hours from Alaska, a passenger in the coach cabin began to cough. All had seemed well until a second, third and finally fourth passenger followed suit. Soon, the odor had been unmistakable.

`"Listen Captain, I think there's something going on back here,"` the lead flight attendant had said. Her call to the pilot was quoted on the cockpit voice recorder. `"It's hazy and people are coughing."`

Professor Jaxon's article meticulously detailed every moment following that call. He described the emergency landing, medical care and even the investigation that followed. The detail was uncanny, from the medical reports of the fifteen hospitalized passengers to excerpts from the final investigation. In the conclusion, Jaxon wrote:

```
"This is undoubtedly a case of organophosphate-like
toxin exposure. The evidence is clear; this is a case
of Aerotoxic Syndrome. It was a mistake for the NTSB
to dismiss this event as a 'chemical exposure of
unclear origin.'"
```

The article argued that a string of similar events were also TCP-related, an outrageous idea at the time. Jaxon recognized the fact that there were competing interests. If Aerotoxic Syndrome was real, the financial loss would be immense. The ripple effects would shake the airlines, insurers, manufacturers and everyone in between. It would be a public relations nightmare. Regardless, he argued that regulators were looking the other way. He said it would be impossible to prove Aerotoxic Syndrome's existence until a sample of TCP could be isolated from an airplane. Unfortunately, a technique for doing so had not yet been found. No one had been able to prove that TCP was definitely at the center. What Julie read between the lines seemed more important, though. The financial losses would be in the billions, and the industry had had little appetite for investigating it further.

Just after six in the morning, the hind gear dropped below the underbelly of the A330 and it touched down at Heathrow's International Airport. To the east, London's busy city center was stirring, and the chilly waters of the English Channel were 60 miles to the south. Tucked into the back corner of the economy cabin, Julie was aching for a shower. The time change was disorienting, but she was energized if anything. Massive airliners from around the world floated outside her window and she watched them with reverence. At the gate, she packed up her bag and filed into the busy terminal.

She was to report to the Strand Campus of King's College, close to the River Thames. The meeting would be in two hours' time and she still had to make it into downtown. She had heard London traffic was a whirlwind, but any amount of hustle would be a change from the often sedated atmosphere of Grand Forks. Despite her preparation, she had no clue what to expect. She nervously ran scenarios through her mind, but ultimately she had little idea of what the next few hours held.

The only thing more chaotic than the Heathrow baggage claim was the morning traffic. The cabbie swerved in the battle against commuter traffic traveling east. Julie had mistakenly assumed a cab would be faster in a town she wasn't familiar with, but after a surprisingly long trip on the motorway, they were now having to cut around packed buses and buzzing motor bikes. She wished she had taken her chances on the Tube or the Heathrow Express trainline, as she had considered. The cab's movement was making her stomach churn, but Julie's focus lay elsewhere. As they traveled over the River Thames, she saw the 315 feet of iconic neo-gothic clock tower rising from the bank. The massive roman numerals on the four sides of Big Ben showed a quarter to eight while spires at its top seemed nearly to touch the clouds. The cultural icon was situated beside the towering walls of Westminster Palace. The structure was dozens of stories high and ran the length of several city streets. At its corners, an ornate tower cut into the sky beneath the red, white and blue colors of the British flag, sparkling in the morning sun. Julie thought of the men and women of the British Parliament that walked its halls. The history was humbling and the beauty inspiring. Movies and pictures couldn't do it justice, and Julie was struck by its power. As a child, she had been a reader; books had been her escape and her companion. She had read about the World Wars, and the terror and destruction people had imposed on one another. Even at a young age, she had been struck by the amount of hate in the world. To picture German bombers flying over Big Ben was almost impossible. But now driving past the immense structures, she was reminded of the fortitude people had to mend and rebuild.

Trying to escape the traffic, the cabbie pulled to the left and cut into a tight exit off the road. The driver honked, a bike swerved, and the cab pulled into an adjacent lane. They turned right, the clock tower now behind them, and drove deeper into the city.

"Look over there, Miss," said the cabbie. His accent was thick and a little harsh, but Julie loved it. Her eyes followed his finger pointing to the right. It was a quick reminder of how far she was from home.

"The Queen is home," he said. Dozens of men in blood red suits were marching in lines in front of a palace. A blooming grove of yellow and red flowers glistened in the courtyard beyond its pillars. The palace was smaller than Julie had expected, but its vaulted windows and concrete crown were more beautiful than she could've imagined.

"See that flag up top," he continued. She leaned to get a better view out of the opposite window. Julie tried to squint at the sun to make out the maroon and blue flag flying over the building. It was big enough for Julie to be able to make out its crests and golden lions.

"It means the Queen's home," he smiled. Julie studied it as they passed the residence. "The Royal Standard flies wherever the Queen goes."

Off the boulevard, the cabbie cut left and deeper into the city. Now among the buildings, the roads were bustling with morning commuters. Coffee shops hummed and newspaper readers filled park benches. Soon, the traffic slowed, and the faces on the sidewalks got younger. It didn't take long for the professor to recognize the familiar sight of trendy young people with earbuds and backpacks.

"Here we are, Miss," he said without looking back. He pulled the cab to the curb and jumped out to pop the trunk. "King's College."

The area was new to her, but the campus atmosphere was familiar. Academic buildings were nestled along the streets, some historic and quaint while others were modern. Hotels and theaters were built between the streets that housed the downtown urban campus. Students passed from building to building, most with earbuds in and eyes down on a scrolling screen. Julie had to laugh; students acted like students no matter what continent you were on.

"Bush House is right there," said the cabbie, pointing. The building was across the street and was hard to miss. He gave a smile but didn't waste a moment. "Good luck, Miss!" he said before speeding off.

The dark letters etched into the building's entrance told her she was in the right place. Its granite walls accounted for nearly half the city block, and its Greco-Roman detail stood out from the ultramodern buildings in the streets around it. Up two flights of stairs and to the right, Julie found the sign she was looking for.

```
              Department of Physiology
```

William Hoffman

"Good morning!" said a woman when Julie opened the door. The waiting room walls were dark, with tall oak paneling and a chandelier that hung in the center. "You must be Professor Sampers." Julie stepped in, pulling her bag behind her. The woman was young, with round cheeks and a manicured bob. "I'm Ms. Ball, the department secretary." She stood dutifully behind a desk, on which was a single phone and an old computer. "We've been expecting you."

"This is a beautiful building," Julie said. She propped her suitcase beside her and eyed the space.

"It was once the headquarters of the BBC," said Ms. Ball proudly. She smiled eagerly. Behind her desk, she opened the top drawer and presented an envelope. Julie accepted it uncertainly and studied the cursive letters on it.

Professor Julie Sampers

"I'm afraid Dr. Jaxon cannot come into the office," said the woman, still smiling. "I know he has been looking forward to your visit." Her nod was polite and professional. Inside the envelope was a piece of paper with an address written on it. "Luckily, it's no more than a 15-minute walk from here."

Julie looked up in surprise. This last-minute transatlantic trip had already been hectic, but it was only becoming more curious. "He wants me to go to his apartment?"

Chapter 21

September 2024 | Carrollwood, Florida

Under the scalding heat of the afternoon sun, Captain Frank Brewer's blood was boiling. His jaw was tight, as he stood with his phone still pressed to his ear. Only moments before, the chief had changed everything. *"We will destroy your credibility, Frank."* Remembering the words only made him angrier. *"We will blame you for this."* It would've felt like a dream if it hadn't been for the physical ache that was making it all real. The words had cut deep, and he recoiled from the memory.

Frank had given everything to the company, sacrificing more than he had been asked to. In its early days, he had been one of the first pilots, and he had paid his dues time and time over. He had worked countless holidays for dismal pay, sleeping in dingy motels and packing his own lunches. When the company had ebbed and flowed, Frank had stuck with them despite the challenges.
Whatever the difficulty, Frank had remained loyal. As the company had grown, he had served honorably. He had mentored junior pilots and flown the difficult routes. Never married, he had focused on his work and had taken pride in what he did. It wasn't just a job for him. To Captain Frank Brewer, being a pilot was who he was.

"And if you come after us, we will fight you with everything we have."

William Hoffman

Standing on his lawn, under the blistering Florida sun, there was something else Frank couldn't quite put his finger on. It wasn't the flying or the six-figure salary that he had suddenly lost. It wasn't the prestige or freedom either. It was something more: something intangible. Turning back towards his house, his fists were closed, and his back tense. Walking through the humid air across the lawn, he considered it all again. He thought about the flight in Minneapolis and his young co-pilot in the hospital. The smoke, the panic, the ambulances, the questions were all nagging at his mind. The fear from that day still surged back up inside him when he was lying in bed at night. He knew exactly what had happened, and the company did too.

Frank opened the back door and filled a glass at the kitchen sink. His house was old, but perfectly maintained. He brought the cup to his lips and swallowed heavily. In that moment, he realized why it all hurt so badly. The more he tried to fight it, the more powerful it became. Setting the cup back on the counter, his eyes narrowed. There was something in the tone of those final words that had stabbed him like a knife.

"Goodbye, Frank."

The cut seared so deep because of what it meant to him. After all he had done, they were ready to exile him without a second thought. He was disposable and, when things got difficult, they had relentlessly dissected him out. For years he had kept their secrets, working quietly and asking very few questions. He had flown and the company had thrived. In fact, the airline's coffers had grown exponentially and those at the top had gotten their share. Sure, he was bullheaded from time to time, but he did what was asked of him. To those on the outside, it was a mystery why Avionica was such a financial success compared to other airlines. But those at the top knew why. Despite the risks, the business had accelerated for years. They were at an advantage and business had boomed, but Frank knew the advantage didn't come for free. The event in Minneapolis had been part of the price. Now, everything would be different. Frank had a duty: he couldn't look the other way anymore. They wanted him to keep quiet so the wealth would continue to accumulate. Maybe he had been one of them along the way, but he would not let it go on any longer.

Intrepid Pursuit

At the sink, he squeezed the cup with his entire strength. Did they really think he would disappear so easily? A bead of sweat fell down his temple. He would not let this company destroy a profession he had devoted his entire career to.

This would not be the last time Avionica Airlines heard from Frank Brewer.

Chapter 22

September 2024 | London, England

The door immediately swung open when Julie knocked. The apartment building was tall and thin, with red brick on the exterior and worn wooden frames bordering each window. A mile from the bustling sidewalks of King's College, Julie had found the address on Ford Street.

"You must be Ms. Sampers!" said the woman standing in the doorway. She smiled brightly and opened the front door wider. Her hair was faded and grey, but she was bursting with life. The woman's weight filled her baggy medical scrubs, but she seemed quick on her feet. "Please come in, dear!" Julie smiled politely and stepped inside. "Dr. Jaxon will be so pleased that you are here."

Professor Jaxon's apartment was a cluttered mess, with books and newspapers stacked on most surfaces. The apartment had more furniture than it could comfortably accommodate. "You must be Mrs. Jaxon," Julie said, setting her suitcase down in the foyer. She was nervous and worried it would show through her smile. "You have a beautiful home."

"Oh, my dear," said the woman blushing. She giggled like a hen, bringing her hand to her chest. "I am Mrs. Harris." She closed the door and stood waiting. "I'm a nurse from the National Health Service."

Julie mirrored her blush, uncertain of what to say. She cursed herself for being so clumsy. Mrs. Harris took a step towards Julie and placed a hand on her arm. "Dear, I'm Dr. Jaxon's hospice nurse."

"Please forgive me…" Julie started. Of all people, she should have known not to make assumptions. "I'm sorry, I just wasn't sure what to expect and…"

"Not a worry, dear," said the nurse. She was genial and her warmth gently dispelled Julie's angst. She patted Julie's arm once more before helping her with her coat. "It's always a little unusual when someone is ill."

"I don't mean to intrude," Julie said uneasily. She had known the man was sick, but she hadn't really thought about what it would be like to visit a death bed. She had assumed they would meet in his office and chat across his desk. She had pictured a personal library and maybe even a fireplace. Like an academic, he'd wear tweed and they'd drink liquor out of crystal glasses. Through reading so much of his work, Julie had developed a fondness for him. He was a giant in her mind and that was what she had been prepared for. But now, standing at his home with his hospice nurse, this felt like something else entirely.

"Dr. Jaxon has really been looking forward to your visit," she said. Mrs. Harris slid Julie's coat onto a hanger and hung it in the closet. "He's so happy that you've come all this way."

"If Dr. Jaxon is not feeling well," Julie hesitated. Something about bothering a man while he was in hospice care felt obscene. "I mean," she stumbled. "I don't want to intrude."

"Nonsense!" said the woman. She laughed and hobbled towards a hallway near the door. "Let me go see if he is ready for you." She looked back over her shoulder. "Please take a seat, dear." She pointed towards a worn leather chair inside the entryway.

The nurse disappeared down the hallway and Julie found herself alone again. Her eyes quickly surveyed the apartment, taking in the scene. A wall of large windows brought sunlight into the living room, where another faded chair was occupied by a snoozing cat. Through the windows, Londoners hurried past on the busy city streets. The air in the apartment was dusty and dry, but something about the space felt sophisticated. Julie rubbed her forehead, trying to calm herself. When she had taken a job teaching at the University of North Dakota, she had never imagined she'd find herself across an ocean waiting to speak to a dying professor.

Buzz. Her phone was ringing in her pocket. *Shit.* She couldn't be sidetracked now, she needed to be focused. A moment of hesitation passed before she pulled it out.

```
            Ryan Rife
```

Julie cursed under her breath. The nurse was moving down the hall again, so Julie stashed the phone back in her pocket. She remained motionless, not wanting the urge to read the message to distract her. Ryan's text yesterday had left her confused and upset. *There is someone else.* She didn't know what to think; the only thing she felt with any certainty was humiliation. She tried to push away all the feelings that the memory brought back, but they were clawing their way forward. Before she could focus on anything else, she needed to see the message. She only had a second. Flipping out her phone, she quickly read the screen.

Ryan RIFE @ 0921: `I'm engaged.`

She flinched, immediately feeling dirty. His arrogance was stifling. She closed her eyes and quickly slid her phone away.

"Professor Sampers!" said Mrs. Harris, who stepped into the foyer again. Julie came to her feet, trying to refocus. "Dr. Jaxon will see you now."

Chapter 23

September 2024 | London, England

"Dr. Jaxon," said Mrs. Harris. The nurse opened the door slowly, lightly knocking twice before fully turning the knob. "Professor Sampers is here."

The bedroom was larger than the living room and kitchen combined. It had oak walls and an immense bed in the middle of the room. Four spires rose, one from each corner, supporting a white cloth that was draped across the top. Fabric shades dampened the light coming from three windows along the far walls, where more books and papers were stacked. Mrs. Harris waved Julie in with a smile.

"You can have a seat here," she said gesturing towards a chair near the nightstand.

In bed, a gaunt man was being swallowed by the sheets. His temples were sunken and his skin was stretched over the bones in his face. The air in the room was still, though the fragrance from a bouquet of flowers on the nightstand hung in the air. He was bald, propped up by a stack of pillows, and had black reading glasses situated at the end of his nose. Despite his frame, there was an unmistakable energy in his eyes.

Welcome, professor!" said Professor Jaxon. He tried to prop himself up higher, but he grimaced before making any progress. "What a treat it is to have you here!" he said. The vitality in his voice was completely at odds with his physical appearance. He coughed a few times before he settled again in his spot.

""It's a privilege to be here," Julie said. She sat on the forward edge of the chair. She didn't want to stare, but he was unlike anything she had seen before. He looked almost like a wax doll with a voice that was coming from elsewhere. "I've read all about you and your work."

The man smiled and a glimpse of a life that had once been sparked in his eyes. "I've had a very fortunate life," he said, looking far beyond the walls of his room. "The world is a fascinating place." A memory seemed to come and go. "We academics are like detectives." He laughed and looked at Julie. His lips were dry, but his eyes still hummed with life. "And it's the best job in the world." Julie had to smile too, feeling an immediate connection. "I'm Oliver Jaxon." When he raised his hand at the wrist to shake hers, Julie could feel the frailty of his finger bones.

"I so much appreciate your time, Dr. Jaxon," she said. Julie had prepared so many questions, but she couldn't recall any of them at that moment.

"You mean the little time I have left?" he laughed lightly. Julie shifted uncomfortably. "My dear." His English inflection was light and musical. "One does what is important when one is in hospice care." He smiled warmly. "When I heard about your work, I knew I needed to speak with you right away."

"It was an honor to see your invitation," Julie said. She finally leaned back in the chair, trying to relax a little.

He smiled graciously. "Now, I understand you are interested in Aerotoxic Syndrome," he said, wasting no more time.

"I've been reading about it for weeks, trying to understand it all," she said.

"And what has brought this topic to your attention?" His eyes sharpened. Despite his frame, his face moved easily with expression. "I understand you are a professor of ..." he thought for a moment, his eyes furrowing. "Aerospace, if I recall."

"I was an airline pilot before coming to the university," she said. He nodded encouragingly. "I heard about an incident in the US and the possibility of it being linked to this syndrome." He studied her carefully as she spoke. "Otherwise, I had never heard about it before a few weeks ago."

"Most people haven't," he laughed. One of his hands rested on top of the other over his blankets. He shook his head, knowing well the world had overlooked most of what he dedicated his life to. "They have done a marvelous job of keeping it that way."

Julie thought about the passenger in Miami and his plea to keep quiet. *"Something happened on that plane..."* She could still feel the fear in his voice.

"Since the beginning of the jet age, there have been reports of curious events happening in the air." He gestured with his hand, but without raising it off the bed. He was engaged but not hurried and started from the beginning. He explained the smoke, the engines, and the history. "People were rushed to hospitals and investigations were sought," he cleared his throat and waved off a tissue from Mrs. Harris.

"But they never figured out what was going on," Julie filled in.

Dr. Jaxon was pleased. "You are correct, professor." He smiled but coughed again. "Finally, it got political." He smiled playfully, enjoying the moment. "A government official fell ill on his way to Washington, DC in the seventies." There was a pause and he smiled at a passing memory. "I had just finished my PhD," he laughed to himself. "I was researching fish toxins and teaching night courses at King's to pay the bills." Julie couldn't help but smile too, feeling the man's charm quickly easing her nerves. "At last, Congress ordered a study on commercial air travel," he said. He looked back to Julie. "In fact, this was the same research council that recommended smoking be prohibited on airplanes." He pointed his finger and laughed. "And you can imagine how easily that went through."

"The report said nothing," Julie said. "The investigation said there was no evidence a toxin was to blame."

"Exactly!" he said, "They couldn't isolate anything, so they concluded there was no toxin." He raised his hands at the wrist. "But what toxin *could* we isolate in the seventies?" He laughed warmly. "Not to mention the fact that the council had very little interest in finding anything."

"A lot of people would've lost money if a toxin were found," Julie said.

"Of the eight scientists on the council," he continued. "Where did five of them get their regular paycheck?" He smiled knowingly. "Rogin Industries." He said the words slowly, almost in a whisper. He waited with emphasis. "The corporation that makes nearly 80% of all commercial aircraft hydraulic components in the world." His gaze narrowed. "Even today."

"So, they lobbied the scientists?" asked Julie.

"Rogin Industries made a system that required lower hydraulic pressure to operate the circuit, saving fuel and expensive hydraulic fluids," he continued. "It was the engine driven pump that was unique," he smiled. "Airlines saved millions of dollars, making them more competitive and profitable." He shook his head. "Money seemed to be limitless, and everyone was stuffing their billfolds. But here is the catch," he waited almost mischievously. "The lower pressure systems sometimes leaked."

"The sealant let hydraulic fluids leak into the cabin," Julie said.

"Precisely," he smiled. "But we didn't figure this all out until years later."

"So, the government told everyone the whole thing wasn't real?" she asked.

"The situation gets more complicated," he reached for his cup and took a few sips from the straw. "The investigation said the *nocebo effect* was to blame."

Julie said the syllables to herself, unable to place the word. She was wishing she had remembered to grab her notebook.

"The perception of toxic ingestion, causing psychogenic illness that is not physiological." He looked at Julie to see if this had registered.

"So, they thought everyone was faking it?" The idea of such a dismissal stung as the young pilot in the Minneapolis ICU came to mind.

"Their explanation was that people were malingering for compensation," he said. "But really they said very little." Julie shook her head as she considered it all. She was worrying that the history may be darker than she had realized. "That was when I got involved," he said proudly. "I was a young toxicologist looking for a project." He smiled, clearing his throat for what followed. "Who knew I had fallen right into the most important problem facing modern aviation?"

Chapter 24

September 2024 | Avionica Airlines Headquarters
Tampa Bay, Florida

"Yes, sir," said Chief Pilot Jett Fitzgerald. He had answered the phone wearily, knowing what was to come.

"Jett!" It was Michael Burben. He was standing behind the expanse of his mahogany desk, leaning over his speakerphone. A vein pulsed over his left eye and his jaw was squeezed tight. "It's Burben." His voice scratched like a record. He seemed to have aged several years in just a few weeks. "Get yourself to Minneapolis now."

"Yes, sir," the chief pilot spoke quietly. He was exhausted but unwavering. The words came out before he even realized what he had agreed to.

"Get to that hospital," said Michael. He took a glass filled with auburn liquor off the desk. "That damn co-pilot may wake up and start to talk".

"Understood, sir," said Jett. He was almost 20 years older than his boss, but power wasn't wielded that way in this hierarchy. To this man, he was a foot soldier. Like a dog, he would obey.

"Get up there and keep his mouth shut," he cut. "Do whatever it takes." The vice president spun the cup in his hand, watching its contents swirl in his palm. Thanks to the results of the investigation, things had calmed a bit, but it was all far from over. "He could make this all far worse."

There was a hesitation on the line, as Jett searched for the right words. It all felt like a dream, with his body in fight or flight mode. "You should be aware of another development." He was glad he had the safety of distance between them.

Michael leaned forward onto his desk, closer to the phone. There was a tense silence. "What?" It sounded more like a statement than a question.

The chief pilot coughed, the stoicism in his voice suddenly cracking. "I fired Frank Brewer."

There was a hesitation, each passing second a heavier force. Burben placed the glass on the desk and came to his feet. "You what?" he said. He wasn't loud but the words were hot. "He knows too much."

"Yes, sir," the chief pilot's mind was racing, trying to think of an explanation. He knew the pain was coming and he could only brace himself for it. "He was asking too many questions," Jett said. He had never heard himself sounding like this before. There was only a faint memory of the steady, confident man he had been. "I figured this would simplify the situation."

"You idiot!" Michael's emphasis was on the second word. He backed away from his desk, rubbing his forehead. He had worked tirelessly for this company since he had taken this post. Through endless hours and sometimes merciless means, he was one of the reasons why this airline was among the most profitable in the world. He prided himself on doing what others were not willing to do to achieve his aims. Sure, there were times when he was uncertain, but that usually meant he just needed to push harder. But now, his inept subjects were going to sink this ship while he was locked in the wheelhouse. If there was one thing Michael Burben couldn't stand, it was incompetence. Especially not when it was his ass on the line.

William Hoffman

"Jett," he spoke through his teeth. "You will fix this." He turned towards the window and surveyed the ocean below. The tide was moving in and the waters were growing choppy. "Because if we go down," he shook his head. "It will be my personal mission to implicate you in any investigation first."

"Yes, sir," said the pilot. It was all he could say. He wished he had gotten out of the game years earlier, before he was so far in over his head. "I'll fix this, sir."

"You'd better," the executive shot back. He took a long sip from his glass. "Because if we go to prison," the alcohol fell down his throat and scorched his abdomen. "You'll be dead long before your sentence is up."

Chapter 25

September 2024 | London, England

"In the late seventies, I was finally getting on my feet," said Professor Jaxon. Julie sat at his side listening intently. "My toxicology lab at King's was small, but open for business." It was a joyful story and Julie was reliving it with him. Mrs. Harris was out making tea and the late morning sun was lighting up the flowers on the nightstand. "I had read something in the papers about a chemical in airplanes making people sick." He grinned wryly at the memory. "I applied for a grant and here I am 50 years later."

"You've worked on this for so long," Julie said. She thought about the stack of articles and the role this man had played in history.

"Long before you were born, my dear," he laughed again warmly. "We went straight to work," he said. "Right from the start there was a rumor that a chemical called tricresyl phosphate was in the hydraulic fluid, and that it was causing the mess."

"TCP," Julie added.

"We had no way to isolate it, which made finding study participants difficult. It took us ten years to figure out a spectroscopy protocol to finally isolate the chemical."

"How did you find people who had been exposed to TCP?" Julie asked.

"That was the exact problem," he said. "It took us years, but finally one of the aviation unions started directing flight attendants and pilots to us: people who thought they had been subjected to it." He eyed Julie over the dark rim of his glasses. "We interviewed them meticulously," he pointed. "We tested their blood and gathered what we found." Julie listened curiously. "These were people at all points in their recovery," he continued. "Some had been exposed years earlier and others only days before," he said. "The data was too messy to draw any conclusions." Jaxon raised his finger again. "But we did isolate the chemical in their blood." Julie was transfixed, leaning forward in her chair. "We discovered that the amount of the chemical in the body didn't correlate to the severity of their symptoms." He adjusted his glasses. "It became clear that people metabolize the chemical at different rates, causing varying degrees of symptoms." Julie thought back to the flight in Minneapolis. "Some people get sick, some don't."

"How did you know it was coming from the airplanes and not something else in their environment?" Julie asked.

"Insightful question, professor," he said, looking pleased. "We wondered the same thing." Julie blushed. "We got onto hundreds of airplanes and studied their chemical environment." He shook his head. "It was a nightmare to get approval to do all of that." He laughed. "I thought the department chair was going to murder me!" He told the story like a cherished memory. "For many of them, we had to buy airplane tickets just so we could get a sample."

"You must've found the chemical," Julie surmised.

"Just about every airplane we tested was negative." He spoke as though he was examining the facts again, searching for another clue. "Except for a small subset," he smiled at the Eureka moment. "These airplanes had far higher levels."

Julie considered for a moment. "And those were the airplanes that people got sick on?"

"Indeed, Professor," he lowered his head again. "You cut to the heart of the matter." She couldn't help but be encouraged by his paternal zeal. "To know with certainty, we needed to be on an airplane during a *fuming event*," he emphasized the words. "It's simply the only way the evidence would be accepted. We needed to see if that chemical was truly there." More coughing came and went. "Even after all these years, we have never been able to do it. It's just such an unpredictable event." Despite the vigor in his voice, Julie could see his energy fading. She sensed their time together was limited. "And that's what the aviation community said when we published our results." He paused. "It's too rare to take seriously."

Another spasm of anger cut through Julie, thinking of Philip's distress.

"We needed a test that could be done on the spot to prove the chemical was involved," he said. "It was the reason why the medical journals stopped publishing our papers. They said we needed proof if they were to keep publishing our work." There was a new sadness in his eyes. "We were conducting experiments on a saliva test when I became ill. I was devastated when I couldn't work any longer"

Julie wanted to tell him it was okay, and to commend him on his lifetime of work, but he looked as if he was lost in thought. He was a dying man telling his story and he had chosen her as his witness. When Julie had started this project, she had never imagined this is where it would lead her.

"But this is the reason why I asked you to come here, Julie." In an instant, new energy seemed to fill him. "Our experiment worked." Tears welled in his eyes. "My lab discovered a saliva test for TCP that works!" He laughed and his hands came together. "My assistants rigorously tested it and it works unfailingly."

Seeing his joy, Julie couldn't help but smile herself. "That's incredible," she said, trying to fully comprehend the implications.

"Don't you see?" he said. He turned towards her, momentarily showing no sign of the pain. "We have a test at last. This can change everything." For a moment, Julie thought the man might burst into laughter. "This could be how we solve this problem forever!"

Finally, it made sense: the urgent last-minute trip, the home visit, and the history. Perhaps this man had a solution to one of the gravest problems facing modern aviation, one he had committed his entire life to.

"Julie, I'm a dying man," he spoke more quietly now and the long lines on his face sank deeper into his skull. "I know we've only just met," he gave an airy laughed. "But what lay in my future has made something quite clear to me." Julie held her breath, not knowing what to do or say. "I need you to continue my work." Julie's eyes widened and she came forward in her chair almost imperceptibly. "Since my departure, my lab has run out of funding and our work was forced to stop months ago." Pain weighed in his eyes. "My team had to take new jobs and move on elsewhere." He tried to smile, but Julie could sense the pain of his loss. "I don't blame them of course. They are young and have their whole careers ahead of them." There was a long pause while he considered it all. When he looked up to Julie, she could see a new intensity in his eyes. "I want to give you this test and all of the science behind it," he said. "You understand the dire problem we face and the power that this tool wields."

Julie held her breath. "I don't know what to say," she started. Her mind filled with all the possibilities.

"You can fix this." He reached across the blankets, taking Julie's hand in his. Time hung in the air. It was more than just a life's work being passed to her: it was a path to solving a problem that millions of people unknowingly faced every day. "Sort this out," he smiled one final time. "Don't let anyone else be hurt by Aerotoxic Syndrome again."

Chapter 26

September 2024 | London-Heathrow International Airport
London, England

Shadows grew long in the afternoon sun at Heathrow. Terminal Three was buzzing with scurrying passengers making their goodbyes and darting to flights around the world. Airy bouquets of white clouds were hanging low in the sky and departing airliners disappeared into them. A breeze blew the sweet smell of jet fuel through the air and, between the clouds, the sky was perfectly blue.

Julie stepped off the Heathrow Express train and into the busy airport terminal with a new momentum. She had come to England with a small carry-on bag but was beginning her return with two huge rolling suitcases. They were dusty, heavy and full of precious cargo. They were stuffed with books and papers from the cluttered shelves of Professor Jaxon's apartment. Cutting through the terminal foot traffic, it was still hard to believe everything that had happened. Her time with the professor had been brief, but crucial.

"Professor Jaxon," Julie had said, with surprise on her face. Still seated beside the bed, she studied him closely. "This is too much," she stumbled. "I..."

William Hoffman

"I understand it may seem sudden," he said as Mrs. Harris pulled the second suitcase of unfinished work forward. "It's not too often one academic gives another all of their hard work!"

"But what about the others in your lab?" Julie asked. "This is their work too."

"They all had to move on, Julie. I was scared my work would die with me, but I needed to meet you to be sure," said Professor Jaxon. Julie tried not to hold her breath. "And now that I have, I trust you, professor," he said. "I have to pass this work on to someone, and you are in a position to do something with it."

Over the terminal speaker, the musical voice of an English woman announced a final boarding call for a Paris flight as Julie passed a family of four searching their bags. A police officer with a sniffing dog ambled casually along a wall and a toddler ran from his chasing mother. Before making for the security cordons, Julie checked the two large suitcases at the airline counter. She made sure her most precious cargo was in her purse before letting them leave her sight.

"In the bag," said Professor Jaxon in their final moments together. "Are twelve TCP saliva tests. They work and they are powerful."

The terminal ceiling cut over the airport's expanse, where kiosks sold newspapers and sweets to travelers embarking on voyages to distant places. A large clock hung from the ceiling and Julie checked the time, walking briskly towards her gate. She needed to get back to North Dakota and figure out where she would go from here. Perhaps Ron could guide her but, for all the information Professor Jaxon had given her, there was no clear map for her to follow. She had tests for TCP, the information on how to manufacture more, a lifetime of unfinished research and new fuel pumped into an issue that had been decades in the making. It all seemed so strange, this responsibility that had been given to her. As quickly as she had come, she was preparing to head back home. What had started out as Ron's offhand advice to find a project had led to an unexpected step forward.

Buzz. The familiar sensation stopped her in her tracks. *Ryan.* He suddenly lurched back into her mind, making her heart ache. Her cell phone was signaling another message from her pocket. She hadn't replied to Ryan's text. In fact, she had not responded to a single message from him since he had told her that there was someone else. Immediately, the bitterness returned. But more than anything, she hated herself for allowing this to be a distraction right now.

She pulled out her phone, bracing herself for more. She didn't hear the overhead airliners or announcements because she was deep in her thoughts. But what she saw on her phone surprised her. It wasn't a text message; it was an email. She would have ignored it, stashed it away without thinking about it twice, but something caught her eye. It wasn't the name - it was something else. In the email address, she noticed the name after the "@" sign.

> FROM: michael.burben@avionicaairlines.com
> TO: Julie.sampers34@my.und.edu

She didn't know who Michael Burben was, but she definitely knew the company. Still spinning, she opened the message.

> Professor Sampers,
> It has been brought to my attention that you have inquired about the events that transpired on Avionica Airlines Flight 1846 in September of this year. Safety is our top priority at Avionica Airlines, and I would like to personally answer any of your questions at any time, day or night. Please call me on my personal number 813-990-9093.
>
> Respectfully,
> Michael Burben
> Vice President, Avionica Airlines

Julie wondered if it was a dream. She read the email again, this time studying each word closely. The vice president of Avionica Airlines was contacting her directly? For a moment, she thought it might be a joke. Maybe some kids at the university had gotten a hold of her email and set up a fake account. She analyzed the facts again, considering how it all fit together. She had sent a dozen emails to the airline early on, hoping to talk with someone, but she had heard nothing back. Given the number of times she'd left her contact information, it wasn't crazy to think they had gotten it. But why would the vice president of a multi-million-dollar airline contact her directly? It seemed unusual. Certainly, he must have bigger problems than fielding a college professor's questions. That was, of course, unless there was something to explain.

Julie felt the weight of the TCP swabs in her bag and fought the urge to bite her nail.

```
Area code 813
```

Julie typed it into the Google search bar. She was excited but deliberately slowed herself down. She could call but didn't want to be stuck talking to some freshman aviation student disguising his voice for a laugh.

```
Tampa Bay, Florida
```

Avionica Airlines was headquartered in Tampa Bay. The area code and the city matched. She stared at the screen, the features in her face slightly pinched. Could this really be real? The implications could be extraordinary.

With adrenaline pumping through her, Julie began to type. She would bite because, even if it was all a prank, the possibility of it being real was too incredible to ignore. She thanked him for his message and said she indeed wanted to talk. She used her most formal text, being brief and repeatedly proofreading before sending it. He should call at any time, she said. She hit send, again feeling the urge to chew on her nail.

No more than a few seconds passed.

Buzz. Buzz. Buzz.

It was the number from the email. Julie closed her eyes, took a breath and leaped in.

"Hello, this is Julie Sampers," she said.

"Julie!" the man's voice played like a big band horn. "It's Michael Burben," he said. "From Avionica Airlines." Julie remained still on the granite floor. "I am so pleased to be speaking with you. I hope now is a good time."

"It is," she heard herself say. She felt like she was in a dream. "I was doing some work anyway." She shuffled towards a bench and managed to get a notepad out of her purse.

"Of course." He spoke with an untroubled confidence that made Julie's spine feel cold. "We take safety very seriously," he paused on cue. "I've been told you had some questions for me."

"Yes, in fact I do," she started to say but he began speaking again before she could finish.

"After I was informed about flight 1846, I was *devastated*," he paused. "Anything out of the ordinary on one of our flights always concerns me." He was speaking faster now. "I directed our safety department to launch a complete..." Julie pictured him waving his hand at the word, "...investigation and to commit all necessary resources to figuring out what happened." Julie adjusted on the bench. "The results showed one pilot became ill, but the captain was able to land the plane safely." Julie listened closely, waiting for his rehearsed spiel to end. "The pilot is being treated and the airline is caring for him in this difficult time." Then he was quick to add, "And his family! We are caring for his family too in this difficult time."

"I see..." said Julie but the executive continued.

"Now, as we always do when something like this arises, we compensated all of the passengers accordingly. We even reported all our findings to the proper authorities. It's that simple: the pilot was sick, and our well-trained crew handled it safely."

"Mr. Burben," she said when he finally took a breath. Her senses were heightened and her hands were trembling, but her strength was growing. Despite his assurances, she would not be dissuaded. "The Minneapolis *Star Tribune* quoted a passenger saying there was smoke in the cabin before passengers became ill. Another source said it was the smoke that caused the pilot to become incapacitated." She was trying to sound poised, but she was a rookie in many senses. She was learning on the fly. "What did your report find about this?"

"Now that is just plain wrong!" His swift interruption made her uneasy. "Our reports found nothing of the sort." There was a silence. Julie was going to say something, but instead she waited. "I think if you were to speak to those passengers again," he said, with a new harshness in his tone. "You'd find that to be the case."

Julie thought of the man from Miami and his plea to keep quiet.

His voice regained its composure after the momentary lapse. "Now I assure you this was a routine incident that was handled exactly per our protocols. And without a single injury." He tried to reel it back with some mechanical laughter. "Now, I would call that a success story if you ask me."

The man was satisfied with his answer, that was clear. He was oily and it would be impossible to pin him down. Even if she wanted to, she couldn't. She was a professor, not an investigator, and she didn't have all those interview tricks that got people caught up in their own words. Her heart thumped heavily in her chest, knowing this was a chance she might not get again. She felt anger rising in her, knowing that perhaps this man was imperiling her profession for the sake of personal gain. It was sick and she needed to do everything in her power to stop it. But she hadn't really anticipated how this conversation would go. She had nothing prepared and nothing to say. Maybe that's how he wanted it, for her to be caught off guard.

"Mr. Burben," she started. It was like she was outside of herself, watching her body from a distance. She was going in cold, so the first question that filled her mind was the one that came out. "If this was a routine incident and there is truly nothing wrong," the executive tried to interrupt but she continued. "Why would you take the time to call me?"

There was a long pause, this one sharper. Julie immediately regretted letting her mouth run before her mind could think. Automatically, her finger came to her teeth and she began to gnaw on the nail. She felt an overwhelming urge to apologize, but something told her it was too late.

Intrepid Pursuit

"I do this as a professional courtesy," he said, breaking the silence. Julie could feel the steam building. She bit at her nail harder, cursing herself. "And I do not appreciate your insinuation."

Julie tried to begin an apology, but the vice president spoke over her.

"If you have any further questions, you can send them to our website," he said. There was anger in his voice, even if he was suppressing it. "I am a very busy man and must tend to other business," he said. Julie sat motionless on the bench in the busy airport terminal. "Good evening."

Chapter 27

September 2024 | Carrollwood, Florida

Frank Brewer sat at the head of his kitchen table rubbing his eyes, trying to massage away the strain that was making them ache. Days had passed since he was fired from Avionica Airlines, and he had barely slept. His anger kept him on edge. He felt the urge to do something, but he was at a loss. He knew exactly why it had happened. No one said it, but no one needed to.

He had been fired because he wouldn't protect their secret.

When he had refused to agree to their terms, he had become a liability. A company like Avionica had no tolerance for liabilities.

Frank hadn't left the walls of his house and garden since it happened. Like a caged animal, he paced so he could think. He tossed in bed through the night and suffered through the hours of his empty days. He had devoted his life to his work. An expert at his craft, he had focused on flying at the expense of everything else. He had chosen his career over family and friends long ago. After years of being on the road, he had permitted reading to become one of the few distractions he had in life. It had become an important refuge from his responsibilities, and he held it dear. He ate up long prose on the history of wars and the politics of social movements, but his favorite was biographies. There was something in reading about the greats, understanding the inner workings of the presidents and leaders who had shaped history, that stirred his curiosity. Perhaps it was seeing the trials beneath the achievements that made them real. Sometimes their stories made him question history, while others only affirmed the way he saw life. On his last trip with Avionica, he had read the biography of Leonardo da Vinci. He had endured the long, dense pages about a man fascinated by his work, a man of countless talents and a myriad of interests. Perhaps one of history's best jack of all trades, da Vinci had been multifaceted and celebrated for it.

Honestly, Frank thought it was a load of shit.

Da Vinci had been an accomplished painter, but he was also an average scientist, architect and too many other things. He was known for his unfinished work and wandering attention. Frank despised the thought. He couldn't understand why anyone would be more than the skill that made them great. It's why people trained and were specialized, to be excellent at their craft. To him, anything else was a waste and a shame.

Frank Brewer was a pilot. Not a hobbyist, not a father, not a husband and not really even a friend. He was an aviator and that's all there was. It was a simple life, sometimes a lonely one, and he would choose it again. But now he had been fired and he had nothing left.

He stood up from the table and moved absently into the kitchen. Rewarming his coffee in the microwave for the third time, he let his mind play through it all again. His face had thinned and the skin below his eyes was dark. It had been days since he had a decent meal, but eating had been the last thing on his mind. Frank had known about the cover up. He had never engaged it from the center but had always felt its presence from the periphery. He knew about the risks and the tremendous gains it gave the airline. He knew what was on the line, but he had never said anything because that wasn't his job. He was a pilot, a man on the frontline, and he took that seriously. Sure, he wasn't faultless, he too had benefited from the airline's gains. It was one of the reasons he made more money than other pilots dreamed of. He had taken the loot without a question and had done what he was told. And honestly, corporate's skeletons hadn't interested him. For the most part, he was quiet and had kept to himself. It had served him well and there had been no reason to change.

But Minneapolis had changed everything.

His co-pilot in the hospital and the dozens of injured passengers were the result of his airplane filling with smoke. The demons swirled in his mind, gaining strength in every quiet moment. Of course the airline wanted him to remain silent because his silence was to their benefit. If they could avoid the repercussions of their negligence, their bloated profits would continue. They wanted to disparage the career he had devoted his life to, and he wouldn't stand for it. Not anymore. Like someone finding an injured animal on the side of the road, he wouldn't let this problem linger any longer. He would take charge. When there was something to be done, he had always been a man to act. It was what had made him a great pilot and he wouldn't do it any other way. With the suffering animal, he would approach it quietly. He would be swift and decisive, taking no more time than he needed. He would raise his boot, grit his teeth and know the time had come. Then in a quick motion, he would end its life.

The microwave beeped and he took his day-old coffee back to the table. His laptop was still open to the email he had been waiting for. He had checked repeatedly over past few days, waiting for the answer he had been expecting. It had come this morning, but he didn't need to read it in its entirety. He had already known what it would say. The *Tampa Bay Times* had rejected his letter to the editor.

The day after Jett Fitzgerald had ended his career, Frank had been fuming. He hadn't been able to sleep, so he had worked. Concentrating his bitterness, he had drafted something he intended to submit to the newspaper. In the article, he hid nothing. He described the faulty hydraulic component and the fumes leaking into the cabin. He knew the episode in Minneapolis was far from the first time it had happened, and he described the incident in detail. But there was one central piece of information. At first, he had hesitated, but then eventually conceded. It had to be said, there was no other way. It was a secret Avionica would be willing to kill to keep quiet: that he was sure of.

Intrepid Pursuit

In his letter, Frank divulged the reason why Avionica was the only airline still having fuming events. In 30 years, it had happened nowhere else. If that wasn't newsworthy, he didn't know what would be. He wasn't a great writer, but he wasn't a bad one. The letter had been detailed and scathing but, more importantly, it had been the complete truth.

```
We regret to inform you that The Tampa Bay Times will
not publish your submission in the Letter to the
Editor section.
```

They said there was no proof. They said that such claims needed the support of a detailed investigation. He needed sources and interviews and, crucially, he needed someone from inside the airline to confirm it all. It was a biting reminder that he was an outsider now.

Frank sat back from the table and took a sip of his coffee. It was bitter and grounds were floating on the top. He opened a new window on his computer and scrolled through the news headlines. He read the captions about politicians running for office, rising global temperatures impacting the beaches in Tampa, and construction on Interstate-275. The words rolled over his eyes, most of them not registering because of what was occupying his mind. The world deserved to know about the airline putting millions at risk for their personal gain. The helplessness was infuriating but the guilt was worse.

Tampa musician and YouTube sensation uses videos to raise gender pay gap awareness.

Frank stopped at the story and thought for a moment. He clicked on the text and read the first few lines. The story described a suburban teenager using a video on YouTube to reach thousands of people. The numbers were staggering. The video had been shared from one person to the next, connecting vast networks until it reached thousands across the state. It had even made it into the *Tampa Bay Times*. Frank knew little about technology and had even less interest in it. He had always considered social media frivolous, but something about this drew his attention.

```
The teen's video has been shared by hundreds of
thousands of people across the region.
```

William Hoffman

Frank sat back in his chair. A few months earlier, he had spoken to a young co-pilot who posted pictures he took while flying. He apparently put them on a website called Instagram and he said it was picking up momentum. He was even making some money from it. Frank hadn't been interested at the time but had to admit 17,000 people "liking" one of the pictures was an impressive number. When Frank had asked the kid how much he paid for something like that, he had said it was free. Frank had found it hard to believe. How was it possible one person could connect with so many people without spending a penny?

```
The video is anticipated to have a million views by
the end of the week.
```

One million. Frank sat back in his chair and rubbed his chin. The scent of his reheated coffee rose from his cup and the distant growl of an airliner climbing out of Tampa International hung in the air. *One million.* Frank liked that number.

He opened a Google browser. Suddenly, something clicked. At his table, he had realized what he needed to do. He had never done anything like this before, but when he had a mission, he would learn. When his back was put against the wall, Frank was the type of man who acted.

In the silence of his house, Frank's keyboard echoed.

```
        How to make a YouTube video
```

A man on a mission can be dangerous, but a man with nothing to lose is lethal.

Chapter 28

September 2024 | University of North Dakota
Grand Forks, North Dakota

The crisp fall air was easing into the bite of winter, and leaves, once colorful and lush, had fallen from the branches. The campus was stirring with looming midterms and the momentum of an academic year well underway. There had been talk of early snow, but it had not yet come.

Julie had been back in Grand Forks for a week and time was clipping past at an unsettling pace. She quietly returned to her lectures and continued meetings as though she had never left. Beyond brief exchanges in the halls or across campus, she had kept to herself. Few had asked about her absence, and when they had, she had kept it brief and avoided specifics. She biked quietly to work and sat by herself at department meetings. She cancelled her midweek office hours and worked at home when she could. Though the past week back in North Dakota had been quiet, her mind was anything but calm. Charged with research and knowledge that could change so much, she felt the weight of her responsibility. What had started out as a project to retain her job had transmuted into something larger. No matter where she went, her mind was endlessly on the TCP saliva swabs locked in her safe. There were twelve of them; she knew it because she accounted for them daily. They were the only ones in the world, and what she needed more than anything now was to get one onto an airplane during a fuming event.

William Hoffman

A few days after her return, Ron caught her between lectures. He was buzzing with anticipation and asked eagerly about her trip. He was an even-tempered man, but even he couldn't resist hearing about the prospect of new clues. He was curious and his questions were earnest. He had always been Julie's biggest ally and she knew she should've spilled it all. Why wouldn't she? She needed his wisdom now more than ever.

Instead, Julie remained quiet.

She kept it quick and evaded specifics. She mentioned the research but not the swabs. She was nervous and unsure, keeping her distance and not quite certain why. Professor Rover sensed her uneasiness and didn't push it. He encouraged her, said she was doing good work, and excused himself when she mentioned she was late. Julie wasn't surprised because she had always been this way. From an early age, she had learned to keep her distance in an unfamiliar space. It was an early self-preservation tool she'd picked up in a broken home. She hated it and knew it had no place in her life now, but she couldn't let it go. Given everything that had happened the past few weeks, she was in no position to shake off habits from shadows in her past.

It was Friday, late in the afternoon, and the faculty offices had long been cleared for the weekend. Leftover coffee was cool in the pot and a janitor was emptying the garbage bins. Julie sat in her cramped office typing. The sun was hidden behind winter clouds and her plants were dry and beginning to wilt. Her laptop occupied the last few inches of desk space not already covered by stacks of assignments and ungraded exams. She swallowed the last of her fifth or sixth cup of coffee and rubbed her aching eyes, feeling fatigued by the piles of work she had ignored. Getting started on it was no use, though. Every time she began grading the first exam or scrolling through her unread email inbox, her mind started wandering. She could hardly focus on anything. She was deep in her thoughts when a brisk knock at the door made her flinch. It pulled her back into reality as though she had been doused with a bucket of iced water.

"Can I come in?" The familiar voice hit her like a mallet. It was a voice that had once made Julie smile but now made her muscles tense. "I'm sorry if you're working."

"Ryan." Julie tried to mask her surprise. She spun her chair towards the door a little too briskly, feeling on guard. There was a silence during which time seemed to tick slower. "I haven't gotten back to you," she said awkwardly.

"Don't worry, Julie," he said. Ryan seemed calm and confident, untroubled by the world. He pulled off his sunglasses, smiled and closed the door before taking a seat. "We're both busy people." He was in his flight instructing uniform and leaned back easily in the chair.

"You're getting married," said Julie. Her mind was fogged by so many things.

"This summer," he said.

"Who is it?" Julie fought a flurry of feelings. First there was anger and disgust, but pain was not far behind. Seeing him now reminded her of the way he had once made her feel.

"Her name is Sarah," Ryan said, not looking away. He seemed unmoved by the whole thing, which cut in a different way. "She's another instructor at the airport. We've been dating a few years and we're getting married."

Julie didn't need him to explain, she knew who Sarah was. Ryan wasn't the only one who worked here.

"We've been together a long time," Ryan continued. He chewed gum with his mouth open. "It was bound to happen sooner or later."

"What do you actually want, Ryan?" she said icily. The brittle wall holding it all back was buckling at the center. She felt exposed and vulnerable and wanted him to leave.

Ryan sat forward and opened his palms, surprised. He tried to laugh but the confidence he usually floated on was deflating.

"I just wanted to see you," he said.

"Don't," Julie said. It was abrupt and automatic. It had become clear to her what this really was. It wasn't love, it wasn't friendship, and it wasn't anything else. At its heart, it was cold and selfish. To Ryan, this was a game.

"Listen..." Ryan cleared his throat, trying to recover. He had anticipated things would go differently. "I'm sorry, Julie." She knew he wasn't sorry. He leaned forward with his eyes still wide and easy. "I thought you wanted to have some fun, that's all," he continued. "I..."

Julie cut him off. "I wanted to have some fun?" Her voice was sharp, and she worried it would crack at any moment. "I had feelings for you, Ryan." A tear appeared on her cheek and she quickly wiped it with the back of her hand. "I thought you did too. I thought we had something." She breathed in short gasps, feeling open and uncovered.

Ryan leaned back in the chair, saying nothing.

"I don't know why you even came here," she said. Another tear fell and she quickly wiped it with her other hand. Julie realized why it hurt so much. "Just go." She had guarded herself for so many years because she had feared what could happen if she pulled down her walls. It was lonely, but safe that way. Of course she had longed for companionship, but she had kept herself closed until Ryan had come into her life. But what she thought they had was anything but true. Ryan had used her; it was a simple as that. He had taken far more than he had ever given.

"I should've told you I was with her," he said. "You and I never said we were exclusive... I thought you understood."

"I shared a lot with you Ryan," she said. Her voice took on a new, quiet resolve. "I trusted you."

"You're right," he said, his voice fading. For the first time, it seemed he maybe understood the wounds he had opened. She had confided in him about her family, about her parents who had struggled with addiction in rural West Virginia and about the strain that it brought her nearly every day. She had explained how she had seen aviation as her way out and how she hadn't spoken to her parents since she had left.

Intrepid Pursuit

"It was just for fun, Julie," Ryan said.

Just for fun. Those words cut the deepest. It was all a game. This was not love or friendship; whatever it was was cold and empty.

"I need you to leave," she said. She looked down at her hands, feeling exhausted. Ryan got to his feet, scratching the back of his neck. He started to say something but instead stayed silent.

Julie had never misread another person so badly in her life.

At the door, Ryan hesitated and looked back at Julie.

"I wanted to tell you something," he said. He paused but decided to go on. "It was the reason why I came here today."

Julie didn't look up. Her humiliation had been supplanted by anger. She needed Ryan to go, to put this behind her and to never think of it again.

"I got a new job," Ryan said. "With the airlines." He looked back towards her desk, where Julie was facing away from him. "The company is growing so quickly, they hired me as a captain because of my experience." Julie had nothing to say. "I'm excited to be out flying in the airlines like you did," he said. The reference to her past made her flinch. "Your stories inspired me."

"Please go, Ryan," said Julie.

"I'll be moving to Tampa at the end of the term." He fiddled with the knob in his hand. "I'll be starting with Avionica Airlines in January."

Julie turned towards him in a reflex, hoping it was a cruel joke.

"And listen, I know that video about their safety stuff is going viral, but I couldn't turn down the offer." Ryan smirked, pleased to get a reaction out of her. "They offered me more pay than I could've dreamed of."

William Hoffman

Julie eyed him, waiting for him to give. This was anything but funny to her. In fact, the past few weeks had already drained her patience and she certainly wasn't interested in jokes. But when he didn't concede, she thought about what he had said. In a moment, something change. The past grew distant and the present more pressing. There was a pause while Julie considered it all.

"What video are you talking about?"

Chapter 29

September 2024 | Carrollwood, Florida

Frank couldn't believe his eyes. In the twilight hours, he was sitting at his kitchen table where he had spent the better part of a week. The lights were off, and only the glow of his laptop illuminated the space. The shades were drawn, and the humid air hung in the room. Stacks of dirty dishes were piled around the kitchen and the trash was overflowing in the bin. He was unshaven, his own odor curling in his nose, and there were heavy bags under his eyes. He was hunched forward in his seat, his elbows pressing the table, focusing on the screen. But in the subtle hue of the midnight kitchen, he was smiling.

It was unbelievable.

He refreshed the screen again, keeping his eyes absolutely focused on the number in the bottom corner. Each second lingered as he waited. The screen cut and skipped before it reloaded. All the while, he held his breath.

42,102 views.

It seemed impossible. The number had been growing for days, but the acceleration in the past 24 hours had been staggering. Early on, he had been pleased when he saw a dozen people had watched his YouTube video and he had been thrilled when there were 50. The video was no work of art: he had never done anything like it before. He had learned everything he needed by Googling. Sure, there were edits and rookie imperfections, but he had finally got it together. In fact, he had completed the whole project in one night. He hadn't even needed to leave his kitchen table.

He scrolled through the page, clicking his video again to watch it for the hundredth time.

When it loaded, his kitchen filled the screen. The dark night sky could be seen through the windows on the left, and the space was lit by fluorescent lights above. Though he had intended to edit it out, he was adjusting the computer camera for the first second. He never quite figured how to cut it out, so it had stayed.

Frank was seated in front of the camera, his upper body filling the screen. He looked tired, ragged from the sleepless nights, but his white pilot uniform shirt was crisp and ironed. He had bleached the shirt for the occasion, and he was glad, because it contrasted with the drab shadows of his home. The black epaulettes on his shoulders had four golden bars and his jaw was square and shaven. The chief had sent someone to collect his uniforms the day he was fired, but he was sure glad that he had decided to hold onto one set.

"My name is Captain Frank Brewer," the video started. His eyes uncomfortably switched between the camera and around the room, not used to speaking to himself like this. "I was the most senior airline pilot at Avionica Airlines." He hesitated and shifted in his seat. His fingers rubbed his chin until he continued. "Millions of people are at risk." He paused but didn't react. His eyes cut from some distant point to the viewer. "And it's time the world knew why."

The video was three minutes and thirteen seconds long. It was brief, but detailed, and no longer than it needed to be. There was no flair, but it was the message that carried the punch. He described, in detail, what had happened on his flight in Minneapolis. The delay, the hurried maintenance, the smoke and the fumes. He described the seizure and the chaos. He had no reason to hide it now, so he dredged it all up. He said this was a recurrent problem, kept quiet by endless cover-ups and misinformation. People didn't ask questions because that was exactly what the airline wanted. But when the video came to what seemed like a natural end, he had one more thing to say. The story about Minneapolis wasn't the climax.

"The Avionica fleet is prone to these fuming events for a very specific reason," he continued. It was nearing the end, but Frank had needed to tell it all. The world deserved to know. "This airline will stop at nothing to make sure you don't know why."

Before Frank had posted the video, he had hesitated. If people actually watched this video, and if they took his story seriously, it could change everything. The allegations were tremendous, the implications even more so, but Frank knew it was all true. The question was whether the world would agree. Avionica would certainly come after him. Though his professional future already looked grim, they could crush whatever possibilities he had left. Maybe his safety would even be in danger. These people were ruthless.

In the end, he posted the video.

Frank scrolled through the comments again before hitting refresh. The urge to see the growing impact was irresistible.

42,932 views.

The low early numbers had made him wonder whether he had made the right choice. He questioned if he needed to go back to the drawing board. But then in the night, an idea had come to him. He was tossing and turning in his bed when it finally occurred to him.

Young Pilots of America.

Frank had created a Facebook account years ago but had left it unused. He had become a part of the social media group after a co-worker sent him an invitation, but he had mostly ignored it. Members of the group posted pictures of airliners endlessly and the content was seemingly infinite. Frank had often wondered how all these people had so much time to waste. And it wasn't just a few airplane nerds either. The few times he'd scrolled through the page, the pictures had received thousands, sometimes tens of thousands of little thumbs up. The group had over 400,000 members across the globe.

William Hoffman

It had taken no more than a few seconds to post his video on the *Young Pilots of America* page but, within a few hours, it had been seen thousands of times. It was shared and reposted again in multiples, making the numbers accelerate by the hour. He spent the coming days and nights watching the wave grow. Before long, he had received a message asking if he would be willing to be interviewed on a podcast called *Airliners Daily*. He had accepted it quickly, and a second invite had soon followed.

It was incredible.

Now, back in the twilight hours of his Florida home, Frank leaned back in his chair and smiled. His lawn was overgrown, the laundry was piling up, and his refrigerator was empty. He needed to get the mail, and bills needed to be paid. But honestly, none of that mattered now. In only a few days, the word was spreading, and he intended to keep the momentum growing.

Avionica Airlines had not heard the last of Frank Brewer. Sure, he had taken a punch, but the fight wasn't over yet.

Chapter 30

September 2024 | University of North Dakota
Grand Forks, North Dakota

Julie's mouth hung open as the final moments of the video played across her screen. Ryan watched over her shoulder, seeming more amused than concerned. When the video ended, Julie couldn't believe what she had just seen.

"So, what do you think?" Ryan asked playfully. He was obviously relieved they had moved on from their previous conversation and his confidence had returned. "I think it's just a pissed off old pilot who got laid off."

The video was as simple as it was chilling. A balding man in an airline pilot uniform sat at a table and said his piece. *"As a proud member of the profession I devoted my entire career to, I wish I didn't have to say what I am about to..."* Her left hand picked at the thumbnail on her right. The man was calm but clearly uncomfortable. He held a stack of white papers with both hands and read his script line by line. *"...but I feel I have a responsibility to the millions of Americans who trust the US aviation system every day."*

How had this fallen into her lap? Since she had returned from London, the trail had cooled. No one had responded to her emails and all her calls went to voicemail. She had a powerful tool in her possession but no place to go and no one to ask. Sure, it was frustrating, but more than anything it was unnerving. Every passing second could be bringing her closer to what she was fighting so hard to avoid. She was stumbling in the dark with a flashlight but no batteries. That was, until now.

The pilot went into remarkable detail about a company's failed safety system. He described a lethal maintenance program involving retribution for those who expressed concerns and punishment for grounding broken planes. He was brief, but honest, and Julie hung on every second. She listened carefully, taking in all the details. It was also strange that she couldn't shake the feeling that she'd seen this man before. He looked familiar but she couldn't quite place him. She saw lots of faces in her job, probably hundreds every week, but this seemed different.

"It's a very conscious choice they make. The cuts save millions of dollars while putting you at enormous risk." The pilot in the video paused and cleared his throat.

Though each passing moment held her focus, it was a key 30 seconds that sucked the air from her lungs.

"...Avionica Airlines has had several reports of toxic fumes getting passengers sick." The pilot looked down from the camera like he was pacing himself before going forward. He looked tired, but it wasn't the type of fatigue that comes from flying in time zones around the world. It was the type that comes from carrying a heavy burden. *"I should know, it happened on the last flight of my professional career."* It was at that moment that Julie finally placed the man's face. Weeks later, and with thousands of miles between them, their paths were crossing again. She almost had to laugh. She had been right; this was not the first time she had seen the man in the video before. In fact, they had been in the same place not too long before.

"I tell you this because Avionica Airlines has become so effective at keeping these stories quiet. A culture of fear and financial bribery keeps it all from being

changed." His eyes were locked directly on the camera. *"All the while, profits continue to soar."*

Julie had encountered this man outside of a waiting room in a Minneapolis intensive care unit, wearing an oversized grey sweat suit.

"The video is pretty freaky, isn't it?" Ryan said, breaking into Julie's thoughts. He laughed and the muscles in Julie's neck squeezed. "I'm still going to take the job though," Ryan grinned. "Like I said, I couldn't pass up money like that."

"You need to go, Ryan," Julie said a final time. Her eyes were still on the screen and her mind was still racing. He lingered at the door, but Julie didn't concede. He had taken so much from her these past few weeks that she didn't even have the energy to look back at him. He started to say something but decided against it. With sweet relief, she finally heard the door open and then click slowly back in its frame.

The sun was setting on the North Dakota prairie and the roads were becoming quiet for the night. It was a Friday, but there was no hockey game, so the campus was quiet. The only thing that moved between the academic buildings was the billowing steam of the water heating old Marifield Hall. It was calm and Julie's was the only office occupied in the building.

Facebook.com

It didn't take long for the idea to come to her, but when it did, it seemed like the only possibility. It was a long shot, but she had to try.

'Send a message!'

Chapter 31

September 2024 | Avionica Airlines Headquarters
Tampa Bay, Florida

Droplets of water hung in the saturated afternoon heat. The sun was beating down on the concrete sea of downtown Tampa and the heat was reflected with a force that seemed to push things forward. The city streets were honking with the bustle of afternoon traffic, but the sidewalks were empty as people stayed out of the heat. Only a few blocks from the waves, Avionica Tower stood under its yellow flag.

The traffic seemed to yield to a black Lincoln Town Car cutting through the rush hour congestion. Its perfect polish glistened in the afternoon sun and its dark windows hid the occupant inside. Once beneath the awning, the car pulled to a stop. A suited man jogged to the car door and held it open like a military guard. From the back seat, the wide frame of a man emerged. His bronze skin was pulled tight under his chin and his dark suit was trim. He adjusted the lapels of his blazer before heading towards the door.

On the tower's top floor, Michael Burben sat perspiring at his desk. He had lost weight and his $3,000 suit was draped on him with space to give. His eyes were heavy and bloodshot. Just an hour before, he had received word that his boss was coming for an impromptu meeting. Michael didn't ask what it was about but the simmering in his stomach told him something was changing. Usually, the owner would direct him over the phone or through his assistant, so this face-to-face meeting didn't bode well. Sunken in the wide leather chair behind his desk, his thoughts were going in circles. He had always been a confident executive, respected by his peers and unquestioned by his subordinates. Bruce Luxton had changed that. Burben had always been king, but Luxton had made him small. It was the truth, as much as he hated it.

Leaning forward on his desk, Michael closed his eyes and massaged an ache from yesterday's booze. The waves of the Atlantic Ocean crashed in the rising tides below, but Michael had not noticed the view in weeks. He had done damage control in companies before, but this was different. Now, he had bribed people with tens of thousands of dollars. He had made promises, begged for favors and hidden things in the walls. The situation was still shifting and was now more complicated than he should have allowed it to get. It did not help that one of his most senior pilots had been fired in the middle of it all. There were allegations, questions and even resistance. To make matters worse, there was the worrying thought of that professor asking questions. He was certain she was not the only one. Michael told himself he had been handling the situation but even an idiot would question that. He could quit, but he knew it would not be that simple. Michael was not the only one who knew about what they had done. If he left and the ship went down, they would take him with them. He had to stay inside and fight from within. In the meantime, he would tell Luxton what he wished was true: the situation was under control.

"Sir, Mr. Luxton is coming up the elevator," his secretary said from the doorway. Michael got to his feet, wishing he had had a few drinks to steady his nerves. He wondered if it was all worth it: his luxurious beach home and the useless junk that filled it; the long hours and the looming dread. Drinking had become the only way to ease his mind. He wanted this to be over, but knew it was only starting. All he could do now was wait.

Without a knock, the office doors swung open in a crisp, single move. Michael nervously pulled at the front of his coat. There was no point fighting back so he simply braced himself for what was coming. Bruce Luxton emerged through the door looking like he was in no particular hurry. He had all the time he wanted.

"You fired the pilot?" he said. Michael was still bracing himself but Luxton was steady. His tone was even, which made Michael even more uneasy.

"Sir, let me explain," said Michael, immediately forced onto the defensive. He could feel the pulse in his temples. "We had..." but he stopped. Uninterested in hearing more, Luxton raised his hand.

"That was a mistake, Mike," he said. He took a step towards the window, viewing the waves. Each lingering second pulled Michael's stomach into more knots. Luxton's shoulders were pulled back and his hands hung in his pockets. Michael didn't dare move. He stood on guard because everything could change in an instant.

"I presume you've seen the video," he said.

Of course, Michael had seen the video. It seemed like everyone in the airline had by now. The chief pilot's incompetent mess had created a tremendous vulnerability and he had left Michael to clean it up. The man who had been the most senior pilot at his airline was making videos about their secrets. It was gaining momentum and people were talking about it. He'd prayed Luxton wouldn't know about it, but it was spreading like wildfire. Michael had figured it would get to him eventually, but he only wished he had had more time.

"We're working on that, sir." Michael was scrambling and the lie burned in his throat. The truth was that he hadn't even assembled the board yet because he had no idea how to deal with the situation. How could he possibly get a video with thousands of views off the internet?

"You've created quite the mess, Mike." The owner's voice was even quieter now. Still facing the window, the afternoon sun glistened on his bronze skin. "This pilot has created a serious problem." Luxton pitched his face up so his jaw ran parallel with the horizon. "He will continue to do so."

"Sir, I assure you, we're working diligently to fix this problem," Michael stuttered. "I have our best people working on it and..."

Intrepid Pursuit

Luxton turned away from the ocean and stepped back towards Michael, who tried not to flinch. The owner pulled his powerful hands out of his pockets and pressed them into the desk. His grey eyes burned a hole in Michael's skull.

"Fix this problem," said the owner. The syllables ricocheted off his teeth. Michael wanted to step back but he didn't dare. The owner leaned closer until his face was midway across the desk. "Fix this *fucking* problem." This time it was a near whisper.

"Absolutely, sir," Michael said quietly.

"I trust you *understand* what I mean when I say fix this." He spoke slowly, so each word lingered. "Permanently."

Chapter 32

September 2024| University of North Dakota
Grand Forks, North Dakota

"I am going to request a sabbatical, Ron," said Julie. She was standing in Professor Rover's office. He sat in his chair, completely filling it, surrounded by books and boxes. His office was always a mess, but Julie found the familiar sight a little comforting.

"You want a what?" he asked. He took off his reading glasses. "What do you mean, Julie?" He had been shuffling papers and typing when Julie had made a surprise visit. The smell of day-old coffee hung in the air and students lumbered past in the halls outside.

"I think it would be what's best for me," she said, trying to sound even. She stood square in front of the desk, more nervous than she had thought she'd be. Julie had been psyching herself up for this meeting all afternoon and she realized it would be as difficult as she had feared. "I need time to focus on my research."

"The Aerotoxic Syndrome work?" He leaned forward on his desk, looking surprised, then frowned. "You haven't said much about it. I thought it was maybe on hold."

"I'm sorry, Ron," she said, sitting down. She pushed a stack of books so she could move closer to the desk. "I know I haven't said much." She was calculating her moves. It was true, she had kept her distance since she had been back from England. Not because there was nothing to say, but because she had no idea what she was going to do. At least, that had been until yesterday.

After seeing Frank Brewer's video, Julie knew she had to speak with him. It was her best option; indeed, she had few others. In another whisk of luck, she had managed to find him on social media and they went on to speak over the phone. As quickly as they had connected, they had forged a bond. They were both pilots of different generations, but their mutual aims quickly became clear. *"These are dangerous people, Julie,"* Frank had said. *"Something has to be done."* He explained that the company had systems to prevent information from getting out. She would find no one to speak to or even to budge an inch. It had always been that way because they had too much to lose. It would be impossible to bring a TCP swab onto one of their airplanes under the guise of research, he said. *"If you're serious about this, Julie,"* he said. *"No one is going to give you permission."*

"You have to understand," said Ron. He was selecting his words carefully. "This seems to be coming out of the blue a little." He rubbed his eyes after a long day behind his desk. Julie was feeling the same way. She would never have predicted she would be requesting time off from the job she loved, but she decided it was what she needed to do. Frank had made that clear to her yesterday. *"You'll have to get on the inside."*

"I understand," said Julie. She had rehearsed this conversation, knowing there would be hard questions. She looked down at her hands and waited. She needed to be tactful and to not give too much information. It would raise questions and perhaps make it even more difficult. Ron was her supervisor, and things like this needed to be cleared by him. Her idea was unusual, perhaps even dangerous, but it was the next step. It would be important Ron knew no more than he needed to.

"If you don't mind my asking," he proceeded cautiously, "how do you plan to spend this time?" This kind of formal awkwardness didn't usually impede their work relationship. She was asking for more than her due and she would have to explain. It was a reasonable question. If Julie were in his shoes, she would ask the same thing. Why was she putting so much on the line for this project? Of course the same question had passed through her own mind. Her plan was unconventional, but it would be what was required if she wanted to move forward. Frank had made it clear that it was the only option. The TCP swabs were the key to this mystery, and she needed to take them to the fight.

"I am ready to focus entirely on this project, Ron," she said. She couldn't meet his eyes because of all of the things she didn't want to say.

"Listen Julie," he stirred in his seat. She sensed his apprehension. "You know I will support you and your work, but you have to understand how this will look to the Dean."

He didn't need to explain because Julie already knew. She was a junior faculty member, with nothing published and not much to hang her hat on. This request would certainly raise eyebrows, but she saw no other way. Frank had convinced her of that. If progress were to be made, she'd have to put it all on the line. There were no more sources she could depend on so she would have to become her own.

"Ron." She picked at her thumbnail as she searched for the words. "I have to do this." Her tone changed.

He exhaled heavily. "I presume you've made some progress then." He didn't press and Julie was grateful.

"I just need some more time," she hesitated.

"Do you plan to sit in front of the Avionica headquarters until they talk?" He laughed and leaned back in his chair. "These people are very good at their job and don't seem interested in saying much."

"Even closer than that," Julie said evenly. She met his gaze and his smile faded. "I'm going to be a pilot again, Ron," she said flatly but it came out with a smile she hadn't intended. "My application with Avionica was already reviewed." The company was growing so rapidly, hiring hundreds of pilots by the month, that Julie's previous flying experience gave her an edge. To keep a low profile, she hadn't mentioned her UND appointment on her resume. "I just need six months, Ron," she pleaded.

First, there was surprise but his expression soon evened. He thought for a moment like he was playing the plan through in his head. "It's going to be a tough sell." He shook his head. "Not only can they not know what you intend to do, but you'll have to convince them why an untenured faculty member needs six months off."

"That's why I came to you, Ron," said Julie. He stayed motionless in his chair. "I'm hoping you can go to the board and advocate for this." She looked up at him, searching in his eyes. "I know there will be questions," she pleaded. "But I assure you I wouldn't put you in this position unless I could look you in the eye and tell you that I think it's worth it."

He frowned and exhaled heavily. He studied Julie carefully, as if he was trying to read something from her gaze. "You know I will always support you," said the professor. "But you have to know you may lose your job for this."

"I have to do this, Ron," she said. "I don't think there's another way."

By the end of the week, Julie had her approval. The news came in an email while she was grading assignments in her office. A six-month sabbatical without pay was news that was both thrilling and terrifying. It was the chance she needed, the opportunity to make a difference, but it also came at a cost that she hadn't calculated. The email included something else that was even more unexpected. Julie wasn't being granted a six-month sabbatical because of her academic promise. She hadn't been approved because of her connections or even her student reviews.

In the era of dwindling budgets and tighter margins, priorities were shifting. Costs needed to be cut where they could, so bargaining had become key. In fact, this chance had been paid for by someone else. Julie Sampers was being awarded a sabbatical because Ron Rover had agreed to take an early retirement in exchange.

Chapter 33

October 2024 | Carrollwood, Florida

"Frank, it's Jett," said the man on the other end of the line. There was relief in his voice. "I'm glad you answered."

Frank Brewer had been surprised to see the number appear on his cell phone when it rang in the early afternoon. He momentarily thought about ignoring it after everything that had happened but decided to bite. Of course, he was curious to know what the people at Avionica were thinking now that his posts were making waves across the internet.

"I presume you're calling about the videos," he said.

"I've seen them all," said Jett. His tone had changed since they had last spoken. "I think the entire industry has by now."

"Why are you calling, Jett?" said Frank. He wasn't interested in small talk, especially not from him. He was certain the airline would be ready to do whatever was necessary.

"I'm calling you as a friend, Frank," said Jett. There was a pause while Frank thought. "I couldn't take it anymore." Frank stepped under the awning of his car port and out of the sun.

"I just resigned from Avionica."

"You what?" Frank said. He was stunned. "What are you talking about?"

"I just quit today," said Jett. Frank could almost hear him leaning into the phone. "I had to get out, I couldn't take the lies anymore."

"I find that hard to believe," said Frank. He was caught off guard and stumbled. "Why now?"

"You were right the entire time," said Jett. He almost seemed to be pleading. "Things are so out of control there and it's only going to get worse. I needed to get out while I still could."

"What are you going to do?" Frank leaned against his car thinking about it all. The whole thing seemed nearly impossible. "I figured they were sending you to stop me from saying anything more."

"Well, that's what I want to talk to you about, Frank," Jett cleared his voice. "If things are really going to change at Avionica, you'll need more people to stand with you. I resigned today because I think I can help." There was another pause, during which Frank rubbed his forehead. "Let's meet in person and talk," he said. "I have so much more to tell you."

"I honestly don't know what to say," said Frank. He shook his head. Things were all changing so quickly. "What do you have in mind?" Some hesitation came and went.

"Let's go for a walk," said Jett. "We used to do that all the time back when we flew together." Frank thought about it for a moment but said nothing. "Let's get some sun and get out of the city." Frank felt a moment of doubt, but wondered if something had truly changed. Jett was a longtime friend, and while so much had brought them apart these past few years, maybe they were not so different after all.

William Hoffman

"Let's take a hike at Green Swamp Park Reserve," said Jett. "And afterward, the beer is on me."

Part 2

Chapter 34

January 2025 | San Juan International Airport
San Juan, Puerto Rico

Highway 26 morning traffic inched bumper to bumper as thousands of commuters made their way into San Juan for another workday. Luis Muñoz Marín International Airport sat beside the sandy waters of the Balneario de Carolina Beach on the northeast corner of Puerto Rico, now bustling with winter travelers escaping the cold. Named after the first democratically elected governor in the island's history, the airport was built in 1945 and had grown to become the largest in the Caribbean.

At the very last gate in Terminal B, First Officer Julie Sampers walked down the corridor pulling her roller bag behind her. Her uniform short sleeve dress shirt and black slacks were cut slim around her hips and left just enough room for the island air to kiss her skin. Bellows of air conditioning fought the humidity, but Julie didn't mind the salty air. At the end of the gate, the boarding door of the Avionica Airlines A320 was open, and Julie came aboard.

"Good morning, Maryam," she said in the forward boarding door. The crew's lead flight attendant was already on board, stowing catering in the forward galley. She was a short woman, born and raised on the island, who spoke Spanish faster than anyone could understand. "Back at it, I see."

"Good morning, Julie!" she said. Her dark hair was pulled in a tight bun and her auburn complexion brought out the deep brown in her eyes. "Did you make it to the beach yesterday?" Maryam lived in San Juan and picked trips so she could be with her young daughter and son on overnight layovers.

"You caught me," said Julie. Her face had tanned after a few weeks of Caribbean flying and she had lost weight, thanks to early morning jogging. She stood in the hallway between the flight deck and the forward galley with a smile. "You know how much I love the beaches here."

"I know how much you love *Puerto Rico*!" she laughed as she locked an overhead door. She swung her hips against the galley counter. "It seems like we're flying to San Juan together a few times a week."

Maryam was right, Julie loved the tropical island. When she had been flying in the past, it had always been her favorite spot. The pace of life and the warmth of its residents drew her to the island, and certainly the weather was a nice bonus. After working the Avionica fleet for almost two months now, she had lost track of how many times she'd set foot in Puerto Rico.

"You're onto me," Julie smiled. The airliner felt like home and the anticipation of another trip brought a momentum that she fell into easily. Flying these past few months had been a treat, and she had quickly realized how much she had missed it. She was once again in the routine that she found comforting and knew well. "I bid for every trip I can that gets me here."

Julie made her way forward into the flight deck and stowed her black roller bag behind the right seat. With her stuff settled to her liking, she eyed the cockpit panel. It was a work of art filled with engineering that Julie could endlessly revere. She loved being back in the cockpit and, though she had not forgotten what had brought her back to the fleet, she saw no harm in letting herself have some fun along the way.

Maryam came forward as her black heels clicked with each step. She was a short woman, brimming with energy. "So, how long were you on the beach?" she asked, passing Julie a bottle of water from the cart. They had flown in the day before and had had the whole afternoon to play. The crew often organized group outings, but Julie usually preferred to go on her own.

"I found some music," Julie blushed. "I was out dancing maybe a little later than I should've been."

"Ah!" Maryam smiled knowingly. "So, you're a dancer?"

Julie leaned against the right pilot seat. "I'm no dancer, but I did have some fun." On the beach, a 12-piece band had been playing late into the night at a bar busting with locals. She wasn't a drinker, but she loved the vibes.

"A girl's gotta dance!" Maryam winked and made her way back into the galley.

After the approval of her six-month sabbatical, Julie had quickly been trained by Avionica. The airline was growing and hiring anyone qualified, making a seat in a training class easy to obtain. Julie had sent her application with her legal first name, Elizabeth, and hoped her previous contact with the vice president wouldn't raise any flags. Fortunately, there were no questions. A company growing at Avionica's pace was hard to keep up with, which was to Julie's benefit. She was at training within a few weeks and in the cockpit not long after. Weeks of flying had passed while she enjoyed the perks of airline life. She kept a low profile because she worried early questions would raise suspicions. It would take time to get embedded, understand the intricate workings of the airline from within, and figure out where Aerotoxic Syndrome fit into this company. In the meantime, she didn't see the harm in dancing on the beach a night or two.

"Morning, Julie," said Captain Cathy Anderson, the aircraft's commander and the trip leader. The woman's greying hair was tied back in a braid and she had three bottles of Diet Coke tucked under her arm. She stowed her suitcase away while Julie climbed into the right-hand seat. "Looks like they're going to start boarding in a few minutes." Her short stature was balanced by her assured demeanor.

"Hi Cathy," said Julie, pulling at her seat to find the right height. "They just finished fueling and they're starting with the bags now."

Intrepid Pursuit

Captain Anderson stashed the cola bottles next to her seat. Over the past few weeks, Julie had flown with Cathy several times and had quickly grown to respect both her skill and candor. Cathy's directness and Julie's quiet focus seemed to mesh in the cockpit. Plus, working with another female in a profession dominated by men was always a treat. "Let me grab an extra Diet Coke out of the cart and we can get started."

Before long, the flight was loaded, and the cabin was secure. Julie had inspected the outside of the aircraft and Cathy had double checked the weight and balance. With the boarding door closed, the Avionica Airlines A320 pushed back from the gate and taxied towards the north end of the field. At the end of runway 28, Captain Cathy Anderson pushed the engine throttles forward and pulled the airliner onto the centerline.

"San Juan Tower, Avionica 44, holding short runway two eight ready for departure," said Julie through the radio. Cathy would maintain controls while Julie managed the radios.

"Avionica 44, clear for take-off," called the controller.

"Let's roll," said the captain. Her mirrored sunglasses reflected the runway ahead. She pushed the two throttles forward, and the whine of the engines cut through the morning air. The aircraft shuttered down the runway until it pitched back and lifted off the ground. Yachts and sailboats ambled in the bay below and the green mountains of the El Yunque National Forest rose behind the wings. The island's north shore curved to their left, where coffee farms and rainforests covered the mountain bluffs.

Gazing through the windshield and over the sea, Julie had to smile. From this viewpoint, the world's problems seemed smaller, and the headaches of life seemed inconsequential. The world was never more beautiful than it was from the front of an airplane.

Chapter 35

January 2025 | Atlantic Ocean

At 32,000 feet, the A320 headed north towards the eastern edge of Florida. The skies were smooth, with occasional wisps of high cirrus clouds. Cathy turned the seatbelt sign off. The scenic waters around Turks and Caicos, the 40-island arch in the southeast of the Bahamas, passed below their nose. The ocean's deep blue hue turned to a gleaming green near the barrier reef north of Grand Turk Island. The premier scuba diving destination was on Julie's bucket list, though she'd need to learn to scuba first. Havana was not too far over their left wing and tiny passengers drank cocktails on the decks of cruise ships on the waters below. The controllers vectored them south of Miami, over Key Largo and the Everglade wetlands before they descended into Tampa. It was a trip Julie had done dozens of times, but the breathtaking views made every time like the first. When they landed, they pulled into the gate and prepared for another leg. It would be a quick turnaround, but that was nothing out of the ordinary. Julie decided to walk around the terminal before they would head off to Houston.

The airport was bustling with travelers fleeing the north for the winter. The restaurants were busy and coffee shops were serving caffeine as quickly as it was brewed. Stretching her legs, Julie walked the corridors alone with her thoughts. Though she was happy to be back with the airlines, it was a rather lonely life. She had grown isolated in her travels as she moved from one hotel room to the next. The flying was a treat, but she had already grown to miss the university. She longed for the connection with her students and the energy that discovery brought. She intended to stick out her mission, she was certain of that, but she just hoped her classroom would still be waiting for her on the other side.

"Julie, is that you?" said a familiar voice. She stopped, wrenched back to reality and hoping more than anything that it was a mistake. It couldn't be. "I thought that was you!"

Julie knew who it was in an instant. "Ryan," she said breathlessly. She turned and saw his face.

"What the hell are you doing down here?" Ryan was walking on the other side of the airport corridor, genuinely surprised. He was wearing a black wheeled pilot cap and uniform, cleaned and freshly pressed. Between them, dozens of distracted travelers were ambling past. He cut through the traffic, dragging his bag behind.

"Layover," said Julie absently. Shock made her mouth hang open. Honestly, it hadn't even occurred to her to prepare for this moment. In fact, she had assumed she would never see him again.

"I see that," laughed Ryan. He walked with the cool confidence Julie had always known. When they were within arm's length, he embraced her like they were old friends. Julie flinched with surprise. "It's great to see you!" he said. When he let go, Julie stepped back. "Since when are you flying?" He eyed her uniform. It had been months since the last time they had seen each other. It had taken some time, but Julie had put all that had happened with Ryan behind her for the most part. Some days, the memories still stung, but she had more pressing things to focus on now. But seeing him again today, it all came flooding back to her.

"It's been a few months," said Julie. Her mind was reeling. She took another step back, physically putting space between them. Her mind was in a daze as she tried to figure out how she could explain herself. Even through the fog,

Julie recognized his surprise too. Before it even started, she wanted this conversation to be over. "I left UND not too long after you did."

"Wow." Ryan crossed his arms, nodding. "You left UND? I never thought I'd see the day."

Julie could feel the muscles in her face tighten. She hoped she wasn't turning as red as she felt. "I guess it was time," she lied, laughing nervously. Her throat was dry, and her mind was racing. She hated how vulnerable Ryan made her feel. In an instant, he could blow everything up. All that she had worked so hard for could be lost in an instant. Julie checked her watch, not seeing the time. "Well, I'd better get going," she sputtered. "Heading to Houston in a few." She tried to smile but knew it probably looked as insincere as it felt. "Don't want to be late."

Ryan eyed her suspiciously, taking all the time he wanted. Julie had the urge to run but her feet wouldn't move. "What about that project you were working on?" he said. "I thought it was really taking off."

More blood rushed into Julie's face. She had just started with Avionica and was still feeling her way around the company. Honestly, she had no more information now than she had when she had started. It would be a delicate process and she knew it was going to take time. So much was already on the line and she couldn't afford any missteps. Certainly not from spilling the beans to this mistake. "It was just time to move on," Julie managed to say.

Ryan's eyes furrowed in thought. He looked like he had something to say but he seemed to let it go. "Anyway," he started. He smiled and laughed, as if the whole thing was a joke. His ease only put Julie even more on edge. "Hey, do you remember that pilot in the video we watched?"

Julie swallowed. Of course she remembered Frank Brewer. They had spoken on the phone and Frank had told her everything: the uncontrolled safety systems and the culture of lies. Most importantly, he had confirmed that Aerotoxic Syndrome was alive and putting thousands in danger. They hadn't spoken in several weeks now, but not a day went by that their first phone call didn't replay in her mind. *"They pushed me out because I knew too much."* There had been desperation in his voice. He was a man who had sacrificed so much to do what he felt was right. *"Be careful, Julie,"* he had said. *"These are dangerous people. They will do whatever it takes to stop you."*

Julie nodded.

"Well," Ryan laughed again. "If you can believe it, he's dead."

Her stomach squeezed. "He's what?" said Julie. Ryan had said it so casually that Julie wondered if she had misheard him.

"He was found not far from here actually," said Ryan. He adjusted his suit coat. "They think he had a heart attack or something while he was hiking. He was found in the Green Swamp Park Reserve."

Julie started to speak, but nothing came. Something buzzed through her while the words sunk in. Things had been taking off for Frank. He had made several new videos and had even been interviewed on a local radio station. His story seemed to conjure up fear in listeners and people were taking an interest. "I cannot believe it," she said absently. They had last spoken a few weeks ago. Besides Ron Rover, Frank had been the only person who knew her plan. It was all coming faster than she could process.

"Howdy!" interrupted a boyish voice from behind them. The disruption jerked Julie again from her thoughts. A pudgy man with a completely shaved head approached. He waved clumsily until he settled on a spot between Ryan and Julie. He looked too young to be wearing a pilot uniform. "Who is this, Ryan?" he pointed.

Ryan smiled but was visibly annoyed by the inelegant interruption. "Julie," he put his hand on the young man's shoulder. "This is my co-pilot, Andrew."

"Pleasure to meet you," said the young co-pilot. His arm darted out to shake Julie's hand. She opened her hand automatically while her mind was still on Frank. "Andrew B. Weber," he started again. Creases cut into cheeks when he smiled. "Brand new co-pilot for Avionica." He was jolting Julie's hand vertically. "And very excited about it."

Julie muttered something absently. She gave him a brief smile, but her thoughts were elsewhere.

"Did you say you taught at UND?" he asked eagerly. "I was standing over there," he pointed, "I didn't know if I heard you right."

"She sure did," said Ryan. He looked back at Julie. Ryan wasn't fazed by any of it in the least. "Not just an instructor pilot either, she was an actual professor."

"I went to UND!" said Andrew. He clapped his hands together. "UND is the *best!*" His eager energy made Julie flinch.

"Well, that was a long time ago," Julie said. She could feel Ryan looking at her, surprised by her reaction to it all. She didn't dare look at him. The situation was making her chest so tight it was hard to breathe.

"Why did you decide to work for Avionica, Julie?" said Ryan. She knew any hesitation would only make him press harder.

"It's a long story." She began to pick at the skin around her thumbnail. She had to get away from Ryan before too much more was said. "When you said they were hiring and paying good money, I applied myself and got a job in a few weeks."

"You loved teaching," Ryan said. Andrew watched on, smiling and happy to be there.

"Well, it was great to see you both," Julie cut in. She was desperate for any way out. "I'd better get going." She took a few steps back. "I don't want to be late for my flight."

Ryan watched her skeptically. As she walked away, his arms were crossed over his chest and Andrew started gesticulating again. She waved one final time before she flipped around and escaped towards her gate. It was out. Someone at the airline knew who she was. Her anonymity was lost, and the clock was ticking.

"Go Sioux!" yelled Andrew from behind.

Intrepid Pursuit

Julie walked faster.

Chapter 36

January 2025 | Tampa International Airport
Tampa Bay, Florida

Over the wings of the climbing Avionica airliner, the flaps pulled back and the speed grew. The passenger cabin was secure but not full, and a mother comforted a crying baby. Some passengers were leafing through books or magazines while others snoozed. In the cockpit, Captain Cathy Anderson held her able hands on the controls, while First Officer Julie Sampers responded to the staccato bursts on the radio. Climbing west out of Tampa, the airliner met the edge of the state and the Atlantic coast. Departing over the Gulf of Mexico was a procedural task Julie had learned by heart, but she was struggling to keep her mind focused. The news of Frank's unexpected death and Ryan's surprise appearance at the terminal had left her with an uneasiness that she couldn't shake. *"These are dangerous people, Julie."* She tried to concentrate on her duties, but her worries were competing for her focus.

"Tampa Departure, Avionica 663, climbing to flight level two six thousand," Julie said into the radio. She adjusted the autopilot high on the dash while Cathy cracked open another Coke.

Somehow, it had become Julie's duty to stop this problem which had been decades in the making. It had already hurt innocent people and more were at risk. Crusaders like Dr. Jaxon and Frank Brewer had been leaders of the Aerotoxic Syndrome fight, but it now seemed to have fallen into her hands. Armed with their knowledge, Julie was on the battlefield and deep behind the line. Today, she had learned she was in this fight alone now. The situation had become even more urgent; seeing Ryan had made that clearer than ever. Cutting west over the ocean, she could only think about how this story was becoming stranger with each turn. Frank's death was untimely to say the least. His videos had been making waves and people were taking an interest. Finally, it had seemed like his message was taking hold. People were talking about it and the momentum was growing. In fact, he had become so busy that they hadn't been able to connect in some time. An accidental death at this moment was certainly for Avionica to say the least.

"That was us, Julie," said Cathy, looking over the panel. Julie was wrenched back from her thoughts. In a daze, Julie had missed the call over the radio. Cathy tilted her head back to get the last of Diet Coke.

"Sorry," Julie said, frazzled. She blushed and fought the urge to pick her index nail. "Contact Jacksonville Center on 135.7, Avionica 633," she said quickly.

Through the windshield and to the left, the yellow outline of another Avionica airliner was traveling in the air a few thousand feet below. Fleecy white lines trailed both engines as it flew in the opposite direction. Their combined speeds and opposing paths made it lock like they were approaching at an incredible rate.

"That'll be us in a few hours," said Cathy evenly. "They're headed back to Tampa for another load." Jacksonville Center controllers warned them of the traffic and Julie responded to them in tempo. "It's a funny job we have, isn't it," Cathy said. Her gaze was still through the left windscreen, looking distantly over the nuanced arc of the earth. Light clouded wisps dotted the sky as the yellow airliner cut past them heading east. "Ferrying people back and forth," she cracked open yet another can of Diet Coke, "endlessly."

"Cathy," Julie said hesitantly. She was watching the sister airliner below too, but her thoughts were far beyond it. All she could think about was fleeting time. "Do you know Frank Brewer?"

Cathy looked back, surprised. "I know Frank," she said. There was a pause while she studied Julie's face. "Why do you ask?"

"Well, I..." Julie struggled for a moment. She was almost as surprised by the question as Cathy was. It wasn't how she had planned to broach the subject, but her nerves had brought the question out of her. "I stumbled over one of his YouTube videos." Stringing the words together, Julie was trying to recover from her clumsy start. "They were pretty harsh."

"That's one way to say it." Cathy shook her head. She laughed, but she didn't seem amused. "Frank Brewer is a character." Julie exhaled, relieved in some ways but unsure in others. Julie realized that Cathy probably didn't yet know the news, but she certainly wasn't going to be the one to break it. "Frank and I were classmates actually," Cathy continued. Her tone lightened but Julie hardly relaxed. "We joined the airline at the same time."

"Did you see the stuff he posted online?" Julie asked, trying not to give too much.

"Of course I did," said Cathy. She gestured, "The whole goddamn company has! He sure has a way of pissing people off."

Julie tried not to react. Would it be this easy? Perhaps the information she needed had been sitting next to her this whole time. Trying not to sound too eager, she asked, "What do you think of it all?" With her index finger, she picked at her thumbnail.

"Listen," Cathy started. "We can all get behind safety," she adjusted in her seat. "All I'm saying is that there are many ways to get to the same goal."

"You think he was too vocal?"

"He's been this way for years." She continued shaking her head. "He is one to keep to himself, but he has also never been one to be afraid to speak his mind." Cathy adjusted her sunglasses. "He has burned plenty of bridges along the way."

"So were the videos true?" Julie looked over the center console towards the captain. She tried to keep her breathing still while her heart slapped below her breastbone. "Are there safety issues the company is covering up?"

Cathy exhaled and looked away. She started to say something, but she stopped herself. The radio chatter felt far away, and the engines purred evenly. Cathy itched the inside corners of her eyes, letting silence wade in the cockpit. The pause felt endless, and Julie cursed herself for pushing too hard. She picked at her nail harder, wanting to take it all back. Closely watching Cathy's response, Julie could only assume she had blown it. Cathy wasn't going to say anything and now Julie had made her situation only worse.

Julie was sinking in dread until the captain pulled a pen from her pocket.

Without saying a word, she searched the cockpit until she found what she was looking for. It was the passenger manifest. The seconds lingered while Julie watched Cathy flip the page over and begin to write. When she was done, the captain studied it in no hurry. Julie didn't move. All she could think about was how she would try and explain herself. Not only to the airline, but to the university when she came back empty-handed. But when Cathy handed Julie the message, her eyes widened. Maybe she wouldn't need an explanation after all.

BLACK BOX IS RECORDING. LET'S TALK LATER.

Chapter 37

January 2025 | Tampa International Airport
Tampa Bay, Florida

In the southwest corner of Airspace B, uniformed pilots chatted quietly in the Avionica Airlines pilot lounge. The afternoon sun beamed through the windows overlooking the tarmac, which was busy with taxiing airplanes and luggage trolleys. The space looked worn, with grey walls and buzzing fluorescent lights. Wall dividers partitioned spaces that had once been used for flight planning, now long replaced by computers and tablets. Outdated flying magazines were sprawled across the clusters of tables and chairs. The smell of stale coffee hung in the air and an old popcorn machine popped kernels in the corner. The room was busy this time of the afternoon, with pilots preparing for the second wave of departures of the day. Many of them would spend the night at two-star hotels before flying back in the morning.

With the airline growing at a rapid pace, many of the faces were new. Droves of new pilots entered every few weeks, though old friends seemed to run into each other here from time to time. In fact, it had been called the airline locker room for good reason. It was where stories were exchanged, lessons passed on, and unofficial wisdom shared. Around 30 pilots were milling about, some chatting by the percolating coffee and others napping. One table held a stack of expired first-class meals and a water cooler bubbled in the corner.

Junior First Officer Andrew Weber sat in a private corner alone. He was new to the company, and the only pilots he knew were the few he had met in training. Even the ones he did know, he didn't know well. He had always struggled with meeting new people and things had been no different at his first job. His brothers always made fun of him for his awkwardness, so he had learned to keep to himself. He had done the same in Boy Scouts and college, which he had graduated from only a few months before. Today, he was sitting alone watching airliners take off like he had when he was a kid.

It had been Andrew's dream to be a pilot as long as he could remember. A fourth-grade field trip on a Northwest 757 had been the first time he had stepped foot on an airplane and the rest was history. Avionica was growing so quickly that they had hired him after a single phone interview. He had moved down to Tampa within a week of graduating and began flying not long after. Sure, people asked him if he was old enough to be their pilot, but he would just laugh it off. He had shaved his head hoping to look older, but it seemed to have had the opposite effect. Life on the road could be lonely, but his parents encouraged him regularly. *"We're so proud of you, Andy,"* his mom would say. He missed them every day. His new life was isolating but he didn't let himself cry. Lately, it had been particularly difficult. The loneliness hung on him like a heavy blanket. All the nights in unfamiliar cities and meals alone were catching up. It was challenging, but Andrew told himself it was part of the job. He'd have to get used to living on the road.

Fortunately, Andrew had had a taste of home today.

In the Tampa Airport, he had run into a professor from his alma mater. Only now, she wasn't a teacher, and he wasn't a student. They were both co-pilots, colleagues, in a growing airline. To find that common link was a treat and gave him a comforting sense of home. He had been excited when they met. He had wanted to talk about Grand Forks and the changes coming to Odegard Hall. He longed for that connection, to share some common ground, and to find stability among all the changes that had happened the past few months.

"...can you give us a moment, Andrew?"

William Hoffman

Captain Ryan Rife, his senior pilot, had told him it wasn't in the cards. In fact, he had made it clear he wanted him to leave them alone. The rejection was bitter but not unfamiliar. He blushed but complied. What had he done wrong? He had retreated to a quiet corner of the pilot's lounge to wait for their next trip. His bottle of Mountain Dew was empty, and a Skittles wrapper was crumpled inside. His feet were kicked up on a chair as he watched another airplane take off. He was alone but he'd get used to it eventually.

"It's Andrew, right?"

The words made the young pilot jerk his feet off the chair. An older man with a grey, military buzz cut stood beside him looking down. His black uniform was crisp and his gaze serious, but the man had a paternal warmth. In one hand, he held a stack of papers and in the other a Styrofoam cup of coffee. "Good to see you again, son."

Andrew clumsily scrambled to his feet. He brushed at the front of his shirt and tried to swallow through the dryness in his throat. He recognized the man in an instant. "Yes, sir!" The senior pilot smirked. "Andrew B. Weber, sir." He extended his hand reflexively but pulled it away when he saw the captain's hands were full.

"I'm glad to see you're out in the fleet," said the captain. A silver mustache was trimmed above his lip and reading glasses were tucked in his coat. "Your training must have finished a month or two ago, correct?"

"Three months, actually," said Andrew dutifully. "We appreciated you coming to our graduation, sir." Andrew was excited and didn't hide it. Not only had the captain been there for his graduation from Avionica flight training, but he had given Andrew his wings.

"I have always enjoyed coming to the graduation ceremony for our new pilots." The man took a sip of coffee and swirled it between his teeth. He was satisfied with the praise. "I try to learn the names and yours happened to stick."

"Thank you, Captain Fitzgerald!" Andrew blushed. Andrew had heard that Avionica Airlines' Chief Pilot Jett Fitzgerald had an office in the Tampa pilot lounge, but this was the first time he had seen him here. It wasn't often such a junior aviator got the chance to speak to the most senior pilot at the company.

"I take it you're settling in just fine," said Jett. He smiled at another pilot who waved from across the lounge.

"I'm having a lot of fun, sir," said Andrew. He shifted his weight and rolled his hands together. "Plus, I've run into several other pilots from the University of North Dakota."

"We've recruited many pilots from UND," Jett said casually after taking another sip. "We recruit up there often." He nodded his head and gave a polite smile to another pilot passing by. "Did you catch their name?"

Andrew flushed. The chief pilot had managed to remember his name from months earlier, but Andrew couldn't recall that co-pilot's name from fifteen minutes ago. "I'm sorry, sir," he said. He snapped his fingers a few times while he thought. The pressure was getting to him. "She was a co-pilot though and..." his eyes perked up and pointed when he remembered. "She used to be a professor at the university!" He smiled proudly.

The captain pulled the cup away from his lips.

"She was nice enough," Andrew continued, sensing a change in the chief's expression. Immediately, he wondered what he had said wrong.

"You said professor?" A new crease cut into Jett's forehead.

"Yes, sir." Andrew sank back under the scrutiny. He became nervous again. "I'm pretty sure that's what she said."

The chief frowned. He looked away and scratched the right side of his trimmed mustache. Andrew squirmed. "Was her name Sampers?" the captain asked. The warmth in his voice had cooled.

"Yeah, that's it!" said Andrew, hoping to please. Instead, Jett said nothing. In an instant, it was clear he was no longer interested in this conversation. The chief turned away and moved across the room without another word. Speechless, Andrew simply watched. He mumbled a curse to himself and then fell back onto the couch. He had only been there three months and the chief already seemed to hate him.

At an unmarked door across the pilot lounge, Captain Jett Fitzgerald struggled with the lock. His hands were unsteady, and dread was brewing. Behind the door was an office, where a desk and a chair sat in the shadows. There was a small window in the corner and a few pictures on the wall. It was a small office, but it sufficed because Jett hardly used it. He locked the door behind him and fell into the chair after the door finally opened. He rubbed his eyes, exhausted and wondering how much longer he could carry on. The loose ends had all been tied up, or at least he thought they had. These past couple of months were catching up with him, and his duties had grown progressively more taxing. He had made some mistakes, he would admit that, but he had hoped things would finally start to settle down. But clearly things would not be so simple. This mess was far from over and things were likely to get worse before they got better. He had had enough, but there was no backing out now.

When Jett opened his eyes, he looked down at his feet. He thought about everything he'd been through these past few weeks and wondered how much more he could take. Beside his desk, there was a pair of hiking boots. He studied them while he thought. The boots were virtually new but, on the soles, there was mud only partially dry. It was debris from some recent business he had been ordered to attend to in the Green Swamp Park Reserve. At least that had been settled.

Chapter 38

January 2025 | Downtown
Houston, Texas

Under the warm hue of glowing fixtures and vaulted ceilings, Captain Cathy Anderson took her seat at the table across from Julie. Crystal glasses sat on white tablecloths while people around them laughed cheerily. Artwork bursting with color hung from the walls and the somber melody of a Mexican waltz drifted through the air. The chic restaurant style of *Xochi* drew customers from across Houston. The contemporary flair was juxtaposed with the mounds of classic Latino art amassed in the space. The restaurant had been highlighted in the airline's seat pocket magazine and had been recommended by many. Cathy had a reservation for dinner and had insisted Julie didn't let her go alone.

"I guess I underestimated how dressy this place was," said Cathy as she eyed the diners around them. They were taking their seats in a far corner. "I should've packed something else." She was in a pink, short sleeve polo and black pants that stopped above the ankle. Her feet were snug in her sandals and her grey hair was pulled back in place. Julie had admired Cathy professionally since they met, but tonight she had a grandmotherly verve that only made her like her more.

"It's amazing," Julie said, taking in the art. Paintings covered every wall with hardly an inch between them. The collection was fascinating, but one stuck out. The portrait wasn't large, maybe only two or three feet in height, but something about it caught her eye. Blue, geometric triangles occupied the top of the canvas, while haunting faces and bodies were squeezed below.

"That's a Siqueiros," said a tall man with a thin goatee. His complexion was warm, and his accent nuanced. He placed leather menus on the table. "It's called *Death to the Invader*," he looked up to the piece. "It's about the indigenous peoples' struggle for freedom from European Conquistadores."

"It's beautiful," Julie said, "I've never seen anything like it."

"It represents the physical and mental strength one needs in battle," he continued. He looked at it thoughtfully. "Really, about the strength anyone needs to fight for something important."

Julie's stomach squeezed. `BLACK BOX IS RECORDING. LET'S TALK LATER.` Since her conversation with Cathy in the cockpit that afternoon, she had hardly been able to think of anything else. Time was limited, and she figured she'd be able to keep a low profile for only so long. Worse, she worried that it might be the wrong people who would realize why she was here. It was time for action and Julie could only hope Cathy would be her lifeline.

"I'll have a glass of wine," said Cathy without missing a beat. Her glasses hung on the bottom of her nose. "Sancerre, please." Cathy showed the same sense of command at the dinner table as she did behind the controls of an airplane.

"I'll have the same thing," said Julie and the goateed waiter hurried off.

On their walk from the hotel, Cathy spoke with a freedom Julie had not seen before. She was off duty and enjoying herself. Julie tried to follow suit, but she couldn't relax. This afternoon had left her unsettled. In fact, the entire day had made her feel off. Frank Brewer was dead, and Ryan knew she was embedded into Avionica. Honestly, she didn't know which made her more uneasy. Her anonymity was gone and she needed information fast or so much more could be lost. Time had run out for Jaxon and Frank Brewer, and she could only hope that it wouldn't be true for her too.

Thanks to the wine, the conversation soon flowed a little easier. The waiter brought a second round and music gently played behind the hum of conversation and laughter. They talked about Cathy's daughter, a senior at the University of South Florida, and about sights to see in Houston. Cathy was calm, and she was clearly enjoying herself but Julie remained focused.

"So, you're new at the airline?" Cathy eventually asked.

"It's only been a few months," Julie said. White-aproned waiters floated around tables holding trays set with impeccable cuisine. "I still feel like I have a lot to learn."

Cathy smiled as she brought the glass to her lips. "You're good," she said. She gestured towards Julie. "You're a better pilot than you think. If you stick around, you'll do well at this company."

"I appreciate you saying that," said Julie. She blushed, trying not to enjoy the compliment.

The captain spun the stem of her glass between her index finger and thumb. "You do have a lot to learn." Julie laughed nervously while Cathy studied her carefully. Julie could feel the woman's maternal zeal giving way to something more serious. Now, she was talking business. "To make it at an airline like this," her eyes narrowed across the table, watching Julie's reaction closely. "You have to be more than just a good pilot."

Julie fought the urge to gnaw on her index fingernail. The energy shifted and the volume of the restaurant seemed to have been turned down. Julie was tense, but she was where she needed to be. She had fought for every step forward on this project, traveling across the world and even putting her job on the line, but she was now at the table with one of the most senior pilots in the airline.

"I like you, Julie," Cathy set her wine glass on the table. "There are not enough women in the field. Hell, when I was in training, I was the only woman in my class." She didn't smile. Cathy was in the lead and there was an intensity in her eyes. "Times are changing now for the best." Julie nodded but gritted her teeth. "Us women need to look out for each other," she said. "This company will promote you as far as you want to go." She crossed her arms on the table, leaning forward slightly. "But there are certain things that you should know." She paused, eyeing her carefully. "You're a good pilot, Julie, but there is a certain game that is played."

The energy between them had changed so quickly that it made Julie stumble. She felt like she was tiptoeing along the edge of a cliff and any misstep would bring her plunging down. Maybe Cathy already knew why she was here. Did she already know more than Julie had realized?

"This company will take care of you," said Cathy. She was choosing her words carefully. "It put my three kids through college and paid for a divorce from my dirtbag ex-husband." She was unfazed, intentional in each word. "I live in a beautiful loft by the ocean." Julie didn't dare look away. "I fly when I want and where I want," she said.

A chill tickled Julie's back. The man in Miami begging her to keep quiet and the ailing man in the Minneapolis ICU spun in her mind. So much had led up to this meeting, so much weighed on this moment. Maybe she had put herself at risk, but it seemed this was where she needed to be.

"Frank Brewer is a vocal man." Cathy leaned further over the table, speaking in almost a whisper. "He got himself involved where he shouldn't have."

Frank's words echoed in her mind. She was suddenly flooded by nerves, and she worked to suppress them.

"He wouldn't stop pushing the incident in Minneapolis." Cathy leaned back in her chair. "He kept calling it Aerotoxic Syndrome." She shook her head. Suddenly, she didn't seem as steady. "He was scaring people and said the company needed to make changes. He was stirring things up where he didn't belong."

"So, it wasn't real?" asked Julie. It was the first time she had heard someone in the airline say the name out loud.

"I said he made waves," she said. Her tone was sharper now. Cathy pushed her empty wine glass to the side. "Who knows what actually happened."

"But the newspaper said something about smoke in the cabin and…" Julie started.

"People say a lot of things," Cathy interrupted. The captain watched Julie closely. Time hung in the air and silence weighed on Julie. Cathy eyed Julie until she gestured to the waiter for another glass of wine. "Now, unofficially," Cathy started again. She smiled and Julie stopped holding her breath. "I happen to know that our aircraft fly at the minimum maintenance standards." Julie didn't know how much longer she could take this. She was tense and the wine was making Cathy unpredictable. "Some of our airplanes fly with hydraulic systems that are ten years older than you are." Her cheeks were pink, and she was speaking a little louder now. "They are old and have never been retrofitted."

All the reading Julie had done about Airbus hydraulic systems flashed through her mind – the diagrams, the pathways, and the engineering. Dr. Jaxon's words came back to her. In his final days, he had explained all the technical details. But of all the particulars she had learned from Jaxon, three words had stuck with Julie.

"The system leaked."

"How is it possible that the airline can do that?" Julie asked. Below the table, she was picking at her nail.

"About 20 years ago, Airbus changed the hydraulic systems put into their new aircraft." The waiter brought another round and hurried away. "There had been reports of hydraulic fluid leaking into the cabins of older airplanes they made." She took sip. "They kept it quiet because it would have been a PR nightmare."

"They wouldn't be able to sell airplanes that people were afraid to fly in," Julie said.

"Here's the kicker." Cathy's eyes were glassy, and Julie was glad. "The new hydraulic systems made the airplanes less efficient." She smiled while Julie frowned. "Not by much, but enough."

Julie paused, thinking through it all. "How is that even possible?"

"The old system had engine driven pumps that permitted the circuits to work at a lower hydraulic pressure," said Cathy. "After Airbus finally switched the systems they were putting into new airplanes, the circuit had higher demands which then needed more pressure. Of course, that meant more fuel."

"So, flying airplanes with the new hydraulic systems was more expensive?" Julie could hardly believe that Cathy seemed to be affirming what she had learned from others.

"Exactly." Cathy's eyebrows raised. "You can imagine how much more competitive a budget airline would be if their costs were 10% lower than their competitors."

"What about the airplanes with the old systems?" Julie asked. "Wouldn't they have to fix them all?"

"When the FAA wrote the rule, they didn't include an expiration date." Cathy shrugged. "If the old system was working fine, they didn't have to make the fix." Cathy took another sip of wine. "Only old aircraft needing significant repair and newly manufactured aircraft needed the new system."

Julie swallowed through the dryness in her throat and ran through the facts again in her mind. "So, what you're saying is that it costs less to fly the old airplanes than the new ones?"

Cathy smiled. "It's not too hard to reason why our fleet is so old."

Fear was quickly being replaced by anger. Julie's hands were making fists under the table.

"When they figured this out, Avionica bought as many cheap old A320s as they could, put some lipstick on them, and flew them cheaper than everyone else." Cathy laughed after another swig. "Avionica isn't the most profitable airline in the world by accident."

"Why hasn't the FAA done something about this?" Julie asked. She couldn't see what there was to laugh about. "It's dangerous, people could be hurt."

The smile dissipated from the captain's face. "That's the million-dollar question," she said. "Literally, millions of dollars. No one seems to know how, but my guess is that money is involved."

"You think Avionica Airlines paid off the FAA?"

"The airline is technically not breaking any rules," said Cathy. "And it looks like no one has been hurt."

"But the incident in Minneapolis?" Julie pleaded. She sensed Cathy knew more than she was letting on. She couldn't look too eager, but she needed to know. She was fighting not to let her anger take over. The information she desperately needed was right in front of her. "Why couldn't they just pull the black box to see exactly what happened?"

"Bruce Luxton is very good," Cathy said. She turned in her chair and crossed her legs. "His job is to make this company money at all costs. If the airplane is old and having problems, it would be pretty easy to make a case for an old black box too."

It took all Julie's strength to conceal what was brewing within her. She thought back to the scene at the Minneapolis ICU. A plastic tube had been shoved down the co-pilot's throat while his parents mourned beside him. He would never fly again. The last she'd heard, he was still intubated in a care facility in Minneapolis. Thousands of people were at risk every day, and it was inevitable for there to be more victims soon.

"Why do you keep flying if you know all this, Cathy?" she asked. "You're okay with this?"

"Look," Cathy said. She put her napkin on the table. "This is all just a theory. Nothing is confirmed." She uncrossed her legs and leaned forward. "I tell you this because I like you and want you to stay. You deserve to know." The captain sat clumsily back in her chair. "I don't ask questions and the company takes care of me." Julie flinched at the casual indifference. "Plus, I know which airplanes to avoid."

Julie coughed on a sip of water. "Which airplanes to avoid?"

"Sure," Cathy said casually. Tables were emptying and the band was playing their last song. A man helped his wife with her coat as a waiter thanked them again. "There is actually one airplane I keep an eye on," she said.

"Are you telling me you know which airplane Aerotoxic Syndrome fuming events have been happening in?" Julie asked.

"I'm not saying anything," said Cathy. She came to her feet and slung her purse over her shoulder. "All I'm saying is that November four three nine alpha is our oldest plane." She paid the bill, and it was time to go. "It's over 30 years old and the hydraulic system is original."

Also getting to her feet, Julie looked away. She was speechless and could only wish Oliver Jaxon could hear what she had just discovered.

Cathy turned towards the door. "There are several old planes I keep an eye on, but I avoid November four three nine alpha because it was the airplane Frank was flying when everything happened in Minneapolis."

Chapter 39

January 2025 | Tampa International Airport
Tampa Bay, Florida

Avionica Airlines Chief Pilot Jett Fitzgerald sat behind his desk in the little office at Tampa Bay International Airport. His computer was loading, the icon circling endlessly, and he was rubbing his mustache nervously. The company had bought new computers a few years back, but Jett had insisted he keep his old desktop. Why fix something that wasn't broken? Now, every second this old pile took to load was excruciating. He needed to get to the company human resources database, but he would have to wait.

Jett hadn't planned on working out of this office this morning. The downtown headquarters had a wood-paneled office with his name on it. Roadwork was making the traffic insufferable today, so he had come to the airport instead. When he had first taken this job, he had loved his office in the pilot's lounge. The proximity to operations kept him close to pilots and he could keep tabs on the fleet. But as the company had grown, so had his responsibilities. His administrative burden mostly kept him downtown now and away from the pulse of the company.

He looked at his watch again and then back to the spinning icon. Running into the young pilot in the lounge this morning had quickly reminded him of why he used to spend so much time at the airport. Despite everything demanding his attention, he had attended pilot training graduation a few months earlier. It was something he had made a point of doing in the past, but he had missed it for the past few years. With growing pressure weighing on him, he had hoped going back this time would remind him of what he loved about this job. Now, he was certainly glad he had gone. If that kid pilot was correct, he had just learned about a security breach that could jeopardize everything.

The roar of an airliner departing overhead rumbled in the tight space where Jett sat anxiously. The icon spun and he tapped his finger. Cursing to himself, he wondered how this all had gotten so out of hand. So much had been asked of him these past few months, but he had stepped up without question. He was forced to; there had been no choice. He wanted out but he was in too deep. He had been all over the country, putting out fires big and small. But what had started out as one thing had spun into something that he could hardly control. He didn't want to know what would happen if he failed. He had given up so much for this company, but he would give it all up again if he had to. Avionica Airlines was his life, his family, and his only future. It had saved him, and he would give it anything.

Finally, the human resources page loaded. A cursor blinked in a search bar and the chief pilot began to type.

SAMPERS, JULIE

He struck the enter key and ached for a drink. Times like these always tried his defenses. Scenes from a lifetime ago would flood his mind, leaving him stunned and vulnerable. It only served to remind him of how committed he was.

The late-night bar, the drinks, the prostitute, the foggy eighth shot, the motel room. Then came the lines of powder, the bleeding nose, and the feeling the world was swallowing him whole. He cleared his throat at his desk, hoping to escape from the recollections of the past. The memory from that night decades ago was still fresh. *The early morning, the hot knife headache, his wrinkled uniform, and the bright lights of the airport terminal. Then, there was the empty captain's seat. It had been waiting for him.*

He studied the empty computer screen. Below the search bar, the text read in black block letters: NO ENTRIES. Julie Sampers wasn't in the human resources database. Was it all a mistake? He wondered if he was just becoming paranoid. Perhaps the late-night phone calls from Luxton and Burben, the constant trail covering, and the endless pressure was simply getting to him. That young pilot probably had no idea who he was talking about. He had probably just been trying to gain the affirmation of the chief. Jett found it grating. It always amazed him what people would do for a little attention from those at the top.

The captain leaned back in his chair and let himself think. The morning after that dreadful night decades ago often came to him. It had changed everything, and he was still scared by the thought of it. *He fell into the left pilot seat and began the checklist. The flight attendant asked if he was feeling okay, then the co-pilot asked him to step into the gate. There were police, handcuffs, and shame. On his way downtown, he blew a point one nine on the breathalyzer before getting into the police cruiser. He didn't actually think the number was that bad - he knew he'd been higher a dozen times before.*

On the computer, Jett held his cursor over the search bar. He'd comb one more time, but it was probably all in his head. The sleep deprivation and chronic stress was compounding. He needed to stop this soon, because he had more important things to do. He'd just check one more thing.

<pre>   Sampers</pre>

He hit enter. But when the screen loaded, Jett's breathing stopped. *Jesus.* There was a single result, and it made his blood go cold.

<pre>   Elizabeth J. Sampers</pre>

William Hoffman

It couldn't be. Jett clicked on the text and his mind kept running.

His head throbbed behind the steel bars of the city police station. He couldn't sleep because the white lights were searing his retinas. He wasn't a criminal; he was an airline captain for Christ's sake. Why was he being treated this way?

"Fitzgerald, there's someone to see you." The guard had said indifferently.

A muscular man stood outside the cell bars in a dark suit that bulked with his muscular frame. His glare was placid, and his eyes cold. Jett had immediately recognized the man and felt small.

"You will get your job back," he had said, his voice echoing in the concrete vault. "But you will clean up your act." He stood with his hands in his pockets, looking down at Jett.

Jett struggled to his feet, making his head throb and the urge to vomit overwhelming.

"This will never be spoken of again," the man had said. There had been a long pause before the man took a step forward. "But you will do as I say."

"I will do anything, sir." Jett was nearly in tears as he begged. Jett was drowning in shame and had never felt so alone. "I'll do anything."

The man had taken a step closer to the cage, reaching his arm through the bars. By a handful of his soiled shirt, he had pulled Jett directly to his face. "You will not question what you are told to do." The words had been deafening. "And if you do, a cell like this will be the least of your worries."

Everything Jett Fitzgerald had in the world was thanks to Bruce Luxton. The owner of Avionica Airlines had taken a chance on him when he was at his lowest. Now, Jett would be loyal until the day he could no longer be.

The computer screen finally loaded. The muscles in Jett's neck tightened. He studied it while the blood beneath his skin began to boil. It was unbelievable, but it was indisputable. He had no one to blame besides himself. He had already demonstrated he was willing to do whatever it took. He was a loyal soldier, and he would do his duty. He hoped his history had made that clear.

Jett reached for the phone and dialed the direct number to the corner office at the airline's corporate headquarters. The human resources file had information about every employee in the company, but the thing that had caught Jett's attention was in the top right corner of Elizabeth J. Samper's file: it was a photo of a face Jett would not forget.

"Sir," Jett said into the phone when the line was answered. "We have a problem."

Chapter 40

January 2025 | Downtown
Tampa Bay, Florida

Amelia flickered her tail as she nestled into her favorite spot on Julie's pillow. The single bedroom Airbnb in the quiet neighborhood of Beach Park, Tampa was Julie's home away from home. Near the Atlantic beaches, the location permitted frequent walks by the waves. Thankfully, it was affordable enough for her to keep paying her Grand Forks lease. Julie had been back from her trip with Cathy for a few days now, but she could not stop thinking about what Cathy had said. Day and night, her mind stewed on it. *"You have a lot to learn, Julie."* Their conversation in Houston was the reason she had come to Florida. *"This company will take care of you."* She had found out a lot, but there was still so much to be answered. Were all pilots turning a blind eye to profiteering at the expense of safety? Julie suspected not. There were probably a few at the top who knew, but now they weren't alone. Someone on the inside had confirmed the problem, but still she needed more. Her job wasn't done yet.

Julie's suitcase was still packed by the door and her purse was open on the table. The only thing she had moved since she had returned from her trip was her precious cargo. She'd flown with it since day one at Avionica and she wouldn't be caught without it. The 12 saliva swabs sensitive to the toxin associated with Aerotoxic Syndrome had been tucked in her purse every step she took. She didn't know exactly how, but she knew they would be a key to this problem.

Her phone began to buzz. It was a call she had been anticipating all day. Julie paced the small second story room.

"Hello?"

"Julie." It was a voice she knew well. Her biggest advocate, the man who had guided her through the uncertain waters of academia. "It's so good to hear from you."

"Thank you for calling, Ron," she said. Julie could feel the tension easing in her shoulders. She wanted to tell him everything that had happened in the past few days. There was so much to say, but no time.

"I haven't heard from you in almost two months," he said. "I was beginning to get worried."

"I found the airplane, Ron!" she said. "I figured out which one has the hydraulic leak." She had been waiting for this exact moment, when the next step seemed so clear, but she knew she'd face questions. "I know which airplane causes Aerotoxic Syndrome." She had many feelings, but at the moment, she was excited.

"Wow," he said with a laugh. "That is big news." He was a curious man, but importantly, he was cautious. He was never one to jump to a conclusion before he understood all the data.

"A senior pilot told me which one is the problem. I have a trip planned on it in a few days."

"You're going to fly it?" he asked. She could practically hear his mind calculating. "Isn't there a safer way?"

"I have no real proof, Ron," she said. "I won't have access to the maintenance records unless I get on that plane. I need to look at the paper copy of the maintenance log."

"How do you know the record will be correct?" he asked. It was a question she'd been thinking about too. Why would the record say anything different than what the airline had been externally propagating?

"What other options do I have, Ron?" she said. "No one else is talking and, if I ask too many more questions, people will get suspicious." She considered telling him about her run in with Ryan and about Frank Brewer's death, but decided against it. There was already enough to be worried about.

"What will you do when you see the records?" he asked. He was earnest but he was asking questions to which she still didn't have answers. Throughout this journey, the next step had only seemed to become clear after she finished the last.

"I'm not sure," she said. She felt on guard, almost defensive, but she wished she didn't. It was an important question and one she had been asking herself. She needed to act quickly. She couldn't wait around for something else to fall into her lap. Her sabbatical would soon be over and she'd have to answer for her absence. "But I know that if I don't see those records, I can't get any further."

"So, you've made your decision," he said. There was a pause while the professor cleared his throat. She thought they were finished, but then she realized that he had something to say. There was an uneasy pause while he cleared his throat a second time. "Julie," he said. "You should know something." There was a shuffling of papers on the line while Julie stood still in the center of her room. Amelia watched from her perch on the pillow. "The faculty had a meeting this week," he started. Each passing second was long and full. "You were a line item on the agenda."

"What did they say?" she asked cautiously.

He searched for the words while Julie held her breath. "They are considering terminating your contract at the end of the year." He said it flatly, like he was reporting the temperature or the day of the week. It felt cold, but maybe there was no other way to say it. She had to sit, knowing he didn't want to give her this news any more than she wanted to hear it. "I fought on your behalf but, unless you publish, they won't renew your contract."

"But what about my teaching? My students do well semester after semester and..." her voice trailed off, as she grasped for something to hold on to. Though she had been enjoying flying these past few months, her job at the university was everything to her. Being there, lecturing and inspiring the next generation of aviators was exactly where she was supposed to be. If she lost it, she didn't know who she would be.

"I'm sorry Julie," he said. "They just keep saying budgets are tight and..." he hesitated. "They're looking for any reason to let someone go." Julie pressed her full weight onto the bed while the news sank in. He exhaled. "You have to publish about Aerotoxic Syndrome, Julie." She closed her eyes, bringing her hand to her forehead. "If you don't, you won't be a professor here any longer."

Chapter 41

January 2025 | Avionica Airlines Headquarters
Tampa Bay, Florida

"Who the hell does she think she is?" roared Vice President Michael Burben. Behind his desk, he paced his usual lap. A headache began to cut behind his eye, like a knife pressing into flesh. The muscles in his jaw squeezed in anger. "Are you absolutely sure it's the same person?"

"Her picture is still on the university website," said Captain Jett Fitzgerald. He stood before the VP's desk with his hands interlaced behind him. After their phone call, he had immediately come across town. "It is possible there's an explanation, but something about this is not right."

"And you're positive that she was the one who came to the hospital in Minneapolis?" said Michael. His tone was sharp, and his patience was short. It had been months since the Minneapolis incident, but it kept getting more complicated and uncontrollable with each passing week. He hadn't slept properly in weeks and the bottle was coming out earlier with each passing day.

"Yes, sir," said the chief pilot. "She was the one I saw in the hospital."

Burben stopped behind his desk and closed his eyes. Anger dripped from his pores and he exhaled with a low grumble. He was habitually aggressive, but this had wrongfooted him. There was stress, there was always pressure, but this was the cherry on top. Something was going on, even if he didn't quite know what it was. He wouldn't let this woman put his operation at risk. He would crush her before she tried.

"How is it even possible that you are so incompetent?" He growled again. "I mean *goddammit,* you hired her."

The chief pilot flinched. "Yes sir." He swallowed heavily, trying to buy himself time. Jett had been asking himself the same question. In an operation like Avionica, such a breach could be devastating. Maybe it already had been. The company was growing at an exponential rate and automated hiring had replaced most of an expensive human resources department. Most interviews were done over the phone and in-processing was remote. The airline was growing, they needed bodies, and this was their solution. "She used a different name on her application, sir." Burben shook his head. "She goes by her middle name and it went under our radar."

Burben massaged his closed eyes. This wasn't just about money or pride. There was more. Michael Burben swallowed hard when he thought about the other part of the calculation.

It was Bruce Luxton.

Sure, Michael wanted deep profits and a growing company, but the alternative was what he couldn't stand. If things went south, he'd have to answer to the owner. The thought made Michael's toes curl. He didn't need much imagination to know how that conversation would go.

"This is a goddamn mess." He turned back towards the chief, pointing his finger at him. His face was red, and a bead of sweat was trickling down his back. "And we can't just fire her either because we don't know what she's gotten access to."

"Sir," started the chief pilot. Despite his loyalty, he had never liked the vice president. Jett thought Michael Burben was arrogant. He was young and cared only about profits, not aviation. It seemed the only thing they had in common was their mutual worship of the bottle, but his opinion didn't matter. Fortunately, Jett had overcome his demons, but the VP had clearly not.

"She has a trip scheduled to San Juan with a layover tomorrow night. Perhaps I could," the chief pilot hesitated. "Speak to her there."

The VP faced away towards the vaulted window, looking over the city. The traffic honked on the city streets below as the pedestrians endured the unrelenting heat. Michael didn't love this city. It was hot and there were too many old people. It was this job that had brought him here, and sometimes he surprised himself by what he was willing to do to keep it.

"Go to the airport," started Michael. He turned to face the chief pilot. His eyes narrowed and he crossed his arms over his frame. He was angry, and most of all, he had everything to lose. "Go to Puerto Rico." It was time to fight, and he would release the dogs. "Deal with her."

Chapter 42

January 2025 | Tampa International Airport
Tampa Bay, Florida

It was unusually cloudy for the time of year, and humidity was making the air heavy. It was another weekday, but the traffic was light, and Julie made it to the airport earlier than usual. Vacationers made the airport busy and work travelers filled in the space that remained. Construction on the concourse was loud and the conditioned air was damp and boggy. Julie didn't notice any of it. In fact, she didn't notice much of anything. She had endured an anxious, sleepless night, and had spoken to no one since she rose. Walking through the concourse, her thoughts were intensely focused on what lay ahead. Nothing else mattered now.

Today, First Officer Julie Sampers would pilot an airliner over the Atlantic Ocean with a known faulty sealant system. She was getting on a plane known to cause Aerotoxic Syndrome.

She wasn't doing this because she wanted to, that was for certain. Nerves made her heart flutter. She was doing it because she saw no alternative. Her palms were sweaty, and she hoped her face didn't give away how she truly felt. In her uniform, she focused on appearing calm. She flashed her badge at the TSA security cordons then cut south through the terminal. The airport was bustling with its usual morning energy. The line of people waiting for their Starbucks curved around the corner and kiosks sold magazines and gum. People talked into phones while others ran through crowds towards flights. As she walked, her eyes were glassy and distant. She pictured the chaos on that flight over Minneapolis. The fear in the passengers' eyes and the ailing pilot in the Minneapolis ICU gripped her. Finally, she was getting to the source, and could only hope she would find what she needed.

The time was being announced overhead when Julie turned into Gate 65 at Airside E. The gate was beginning to fill with early passengers, but the agent counter was vacant. The plane wouldn't start boarding for over a half an hour, but Julie needed every one of those minutes. It would be a full flight, 153 people to be exact, with a route over hundreds of miles of warm salty sea. The flight today would bring her yet again to San Juan, Puerto Rico, but she wasn't focused on the destination. She was focused only on the journey. So much was riding on this moment – the research, the job she loved, her future – but she'd have to get to San Juan and back safely first.

Before she made her way down the gate, she looked closely at the ship at the end of the bridge. November four three nine alpha looked like any other A320 Julie had ever flown. She studied it for only a second because she had seen all she needed to see. Hazard yellow paint covered it from nose to tail and black, block letters spelled the company's name along the fuselage. The Avionica seal, black and round, was stuck on the tail. The paint was clean and new, but Julie knew it covered up old bones. The livery was hideous, but Avionica's flights weren't full because of their paint job. They were full because of the dirt-cheap fares. Unfortunately, it seemed only Julie knew the true price people were paying.

The plane had been built before Julie was born. It certainly was not uncommon for an airliner to be a decade or two old, but this was on the distant end of the spectrum. Over 100,000 flight hours had been logged in it and it had completed over 20,000 flights. She knew this because she had spent the prior afternoon Googling. Plenty of information could be found online, even about the oldest airplanes. FAA records were publicly available, and a simple internet search of the airplane's tail number revealed plenty. Julie had intended to learn as much as she could before she stepped foot on board. Before it joined the Avionica fleet, it had been owned by over five other airlines including three overseas. Renovated could mean many things, but Julie guessed it had probably stopped at the paint. What wasn't online was the information that she really needed. Meticulous maintenance records had to be kept on every aircraft, but of course those weren't readily available with a simple internet search. Julie couldn't ask the company for them either. Why would a junior pilot need remote access to those? At Avionica, only captains had electronic access to maintenance records because they had to approve airworthiness prior to a flight. It would raise questions that she didn't want to answer if she pursued that access. Instead, Julie would have to get them from the one place that she could. If she wanted the truth, she'd have to get the records herself.

Julie presented her badge at the jet bridge door and it unlocked with a click. She closed it behind her, feeling the eyes of nosy passengers watching. Her movements felt clumsy, and her bag got stuck in the door. She struggled until it relented, then she hurried down the bridge. She was anxious, like she had an audience for a crime. Of course, she knew it was ridiculous. There was nothing unusual, it was all in her head. Sure, she was early, but that was the sign of a diligent pilot, not a sleuth. As she walked down the jet bridge, she closed her eyes and exhaled. If she were going to get through this, she'd have to keep her cool.

The airplane was empty and ready for a trip. The cabin lights were on and the plane was fully stocked. The rows of economy seats were cramped together, and the galleys were small to accommodate more seats. The aisle was narrow and the luggage bins tiny. The interior seemed unremarkable, like any other modern low-cost airline, but Julie knew better.

Between these walls, something sinister had happened. The façade was convincing, but Julie knew the truth.

The smoke. The coughing. The dizziness. The panic. Being in this spot pulled Julie deep into her thoughts. Looking over the sea of empty seats, the fear that had once been here was not hard to imagine.

The maintenance records.

Time was limited and Julie needed to get them while she could be alone in the cockpit. It would be hard to explain why she was snapping pictures of the maintenance records with her cell phone if someone were to ask.

Julie cut into the cockpit and stashed her suitcase in the closet. Her heart was racing and her abdomen tight. She picked her thumbnail with her front incisor, letting the old habit ease her nerves. It all rested on this moment. If Julie was correct, these records would give her proof that Aerotoxic Syndrome was indeed alive. No one could deny it anymore, no matter how much money was on the line.

```
AIRCRAFT MAINTENANCE RECORDS
```

Behind the center console, three large binders were stashed in a cubby. The letters were clear and bold, like evidence hiding in plain sight. It was the file she'd been waiting to see. Julie peered back through the cockpit door before she grabbed the first hardcover binder. She jumped quickly into the co-pilot seat and urgently began leafing through it.

There was a specific date she was looking for and she knew it by heart.

```
September 2024
```

Julie found the section and began skimming furiously. Through the boarding door, she heard one of the ground crew working in the gate and a luggage door below the plane open.

Her target was the sixth of September. That was the day when smoke had filled this airplane and Frank Brewer had made an emergency landing. If there was any maintenance action taken before or after that flight, it would have been documented in the records. From a changed cockpit light to a new engine installed, every fix should be detailed. It was the law and for good reason. With ever-changing pilots and ground crews, it was a form of reassurance. Before a pilot left the ground, they could feel confident the plane was safe. It was a system that worked. That was, of course, dependent wholly on one thing: whether the maintenance records were accurate.

```
0730 September 6, 2024
```

Julie found the page. There was a maintenance entry on the day of the event. Her stomach dropped.

```
Low hydraulic pressure warning in yellow reservoir.
Low fluid refilled to specified level. Sufficient
pressure generated after operational equipment
check.
```

The handwritten notes were scribbled, and smears of oil stained the page. Julie squinted, bringing her face closer to the book. Eventually, she made out the words. She recalled Frank mentioning the trip had been delayed because of maintenance and now she had found it logged in the records. There had been low hydraulic pressure, and the ground crew was called in. They checked the system and added more fluid. Frank must have felt assured enough to fly it full of people but certainly he must have known the possibilities. Julie's mind recalled the complicated diagrams and flowcharts of the airplane's systems. Why had the fluid been low? She was piecing it together, feeling each second pass. Did the company know this was documented? Julie read on, finding another note from later in the day.

```
2130 September 6, 2024
```

```
Low hydraulic fluid warning. Presumed leak
secondary to sealant failure adjacent to engine
driven pump. Inspected and repaired. Fluid
replenished and passed operational pressure check.
```

"Jesus," Julie said to herself. She again bit into her nail, making it bleed. It was all coming together, but she could hardly believe it. She looked at the time again. 2130. The notes written were from later that night, well after the fuming event that had brought the plane back to Minneapolis. By the time this note had been written, the plane was empty, the news crews had come, and people were in the hospital. The notes were vague, but they held what she needed.

There had been a hole. The hydraulic system had been leaking fluid into the cabin. Fluid had been escaping and that was why the level had been low. Aerotoxic Syndrome had occurred in this airplane in the exact way that Jaxon had described it. But instead of fixing the problem, the airline had done a limited repair and kept flying. Why would they change it? It was clear what a new hydraulic system would mean. Now, Julie was holding the information that she had desperately needed.

Behind her, three flight attendants boarded in the forward galley. One said something Julie couldn't make out and the others laughed. In the back of the plane, more cases of soda were being loaded. Soon, passengers would flood the plane ready for San Juan. There wasn't much more time.

Julie pulled her phone out of her pocket. She fumbled with it, her nerves making her fingers clumsy, but she finally began snapping photos. She got the cover, where the airplane's information was listed, and each of the key pages. When she had it all, she closed the book. She fell back into the co-pilot's seat and swallowed despite her dry throat. The tension in her shoulders relaxed and she exhaled. Finally, it felt like a step forward. In all of this mess, it suddenly seemed like there was some clarity in the fog. Hydraulic fluid had leaked into the cabin that day. It was all in the records. She had her proof.

Maybe she was actually going to make a difference.

Julie was going to stash the book back in its place, but before she did, she thought she'd look at one more thing. She paged forward, passing six months of notes. She skimmed them, noting simple fixes like lavatory lights and cabin seats. Really since the incident, not much had happened. She relaxed a little. Since September, there had been no major issues documented. The thought calmed her nerves, given that she was about to fly this plane full of people over the ocean.

But before she closed the black hardcover book, one more thing caught her eye. The tension returned to her shoulders, this time with a tighter squeeze.

It was the final page. The words held her by the throat and wouldn't let go. She read them again, letting it sink in. There was a final entry in the logbook. It wasn't from long ago; in fact it was from ten hours earlier.

```
2100 January 19, 2025
```

The record didn't describe a simple fix. It wasn't a switch of a light bulb or lavatory lock. The boarding door hadn't required greasing and an overhead bin hadn't needed to be repaired. Instead, there was an eerie symmetry to the entry because she knew exactly what the fix would be.

```
Low hydraulic fluid level in the yellow reservoir.
Refilled and pressure generated was sufficient. Ops
check good.
```

Ground crews had filled the hydraulic fluid because the pressure was low. Not months ago, but only hours.

There is a leak.

"Hi Julie!"

Julie was startled, but recognized the voice in an instant. It wrenched her from her thoughts, like a scream dragging her from sleep.

"We're on the same trip!"

Julie closed the book and twisted away from the cockpit panel. There in the forward door, Ryan stood with his eyes bright and wide. He was wearing the white and black uniform of the airline and his bag was rolling behind him. Four golden bars were embroidered on his sleeve and his smile was broad.

"Surprise!" He laughed and came forward into the cockpit.

Chapter 43

January 2025 | Tampa International Airport
Tampa Bay, Florida

"What are you doing here?" Julie's words came out like a cough.

"Well, nice to see you too, Julie," Ryan laughed, unbothered. He tucked his suitcase away and tossed a stack of papers on the left seat.

"Wait," Julie asked while her mind cut through the fog. "Are you flying this trip?" She quickly tucked the record book back in its place.

"You're not happy to see me?" Ryan asked facetiously. He jumped into the left captain's seat using the handle on the dash. His presence immediately made the space feel smaller. "I saw that this flight needed a captain. When I saw your name on the list, I decided to pick it up!" He sounded assured, and Julie felt sick. She had nothing to say. Her palms were sweaty, and her feet were cold. She started to bring another fingernail to her teeth, but she stopped herself. In any other place, waves of anger would be crashing over her. She hated it, remembering what he did to her. But today, she couldn't afford distractions.

"Isn't this fun?" Ryan laughed and Julie felt suffocated. The captain adjusted his seat with a cocky smirk. "It's like old times," he looked over. "I thought we could catch up."

She couldn't get herself to look at him. Looking through the right window, she closed her eyes and tried to collect herself. What could she tell him? Certainly, Ryan would have questions. Why had she left UND? What about her classes and students? Worse yet, he would bring up the research. *Aerotoxic Syndrome.* They hadn't spoken since the last time they had run into each other at the Tampa terminal. Now, stuck in this cockpit with him, she was worried that there would be questions she didn't dare answer. *They are recording every word.* Julie remembered Cathy gesturing to the cockpit black box.

"You are certainly thorough," Ryan said, pointing to the maintenance records. Amused, he shook his head. Julie turned white. "Everything look up to speed?"

Julie tried to look unperturbed, but she was uncomfortable for many reasons. She thought about the pictures on her phone. "I didn't look too closely," she lied. Worry and fear were spinning round in her mind. *There's a leak.*

Ryan began shuffling through his papers. He adjusted his seat again and flipped on his sunglasses. All the while, Julie was trying to figure out what to do. The fear was real, and it was hard for her to fight the urge to say something. *There's a leak.* She thought about the chaos and fear over Minneapolis. The white smoke filling the cabin and the panic it had caused. *"He was stirring things up where he didn't belong."*

"There is actually something in the records that I'm concerned about." Julie's fear finally overpowered her hesitation. Her cheeks were hot with blood. The internal battle was making her vulnerable, and her fingernail eventually came to her teeth. "Looks like they repaired a leak in the yellow hydraulic reservoir and…" her voice trailed off.

"It's repaired, right?" Ryan didn't look up. He was unconcerned, and most of all, he was arrogantly sure of himself. He turned the next page, focused on their departure paperwork. "I think this plane came right from maintenance."

"Right…" Julie kept gnawing on her nail. Her mind reeled, trying to think of what to say. She knew too much. "I have just…" she hesitated again. "Heard about issues with this plane and the hydraulics." She thought about what Cathy Anderson had said about the safety culture and why the fleet was so old. She didn't dare say why she had left UND to come to this company. Most importantly, she didn't say how afraid she was to fly this airplane. But what she couldn't keep silent about was what she saw in the maintenance records.

"If maintenance signed off," Ryan said, scrolling through his phone. "Then we are all set." He tucked it into his shirt pocket. "Let's get started."

"Really, Ryan," Julie started. "I'm not so sure that…" But she was not able to finish.

"Julie," Ryan's voice was sharper now. "If maintenance said we're good to go," he eyed her across the console, "then we're good to go."

"Ryan, I'm serious," Julie pushed. Ryan's jaw tightened. "I really think there is something we should talk about." Ryan put his hand up to stop her while she thought of all the people filing aboard.

"There is no reason for this plane to not leave exactly on time," he said. He pulled off his sunglasses. "If this flight is late, I will lose the bonus." His sudden harshness took Julie off guard. "You know how this works." He flipped his sunglasses on again and tried to bring about a lighter mood with a laugh. "Now close the door and let's get started."

At the head of the active runway at Tampa Bay International Airport, Avionica Airline's oldest A320 stood ready for departure. Captain Ryan Rife and First Officer Julie Sampers sat at the controls as they completed their final pre-flight checks. The engines idled and the cabin was secure. With the final checklists completed, Ryan pulled the aircraft onto the runway and slowed it to a stop.

Julie's heart was racing and her vision was narrow. She felt light-headed, thanks to her quick shallow breathing. Trying to remain calm, she thought of all the things that could go wrong in the next few moments. She wanted to delay the departure, to use any excuse she could to keep this airplane on the ground. She could quit this job forever and get back to her classroom. With the information she had, she could write a paper and hope that someone else would connect the final dots. Sitting at the head of the active runway, she wanted out, and she wanted it now. And while everything could very well be fine as Ryan had said, she could not help but worry about all the similarities. As the tower cleared them for take-off, something else occurred to Julie. Something worse than Julie could have ever foreseen. In acquiescing to this departure, Julie realized that she too was exposing people to the risk that she had been trying so hard to rectify.

"We're cleared," said Ryan looking at his watch. "Let's go."

He pushed the throttles forward and the engine's volume began to grow. The aircraft shuttered down the runway with steady acceleration. At 165 knots, Ryan pulled back on the sidestick and the nose came off the ground. In less than a second, the main landing gear came off the earth and lifted up toward the sky.

Julie had never been one to pray. Life had taught her that no God would allow the cruelty and evil that existed in the world. But now climbing over the Atlantic Ocean, Julie pleaded silently to anyone who might be listening to her prayer.

Chapter 44

January 2025 | Best Western Hotel
San Juan, Puerto Rico

Jett Fitzgerald emerged from a yellow cab into the humid island air. Bell boys hustled with luggage carts and the island sun burst through the cloudless sky. The Afro-Cuban beat of Mark Anthony's guitar strings in *Preciosa* buzzed under the hotel awning and a warm island breeze made collars flip and dresses swirl. His casual appearance, a tropical shirt unbuttoned low and khaki fedora, was at odds with his focus. He had been to this Best Western dozens of times. He surveyed the travelers around him, fat and sunburnt, from behind the dark lenses of his sunglasses. Mountains, green and lush with rich vegetation, peaked to the west and birds sung in a tropical symphony. He loved Puerto Rico. Back when he had been drinking, he had loved it even more.

Today, he was in a stoic frame of mind. He had been called to arms, and he was ready.

Walking through the automatic sliding doors, he entered the hotel. It was far from lavish, quite modest in fact, but it was clean and it served its purpose. To Jett, it was like a familiar second home. In fact, it was that way for most pilots in the company. This Best Western was where the airline always housed a crew on a layover in San Juan.

"Room 232, Mr. Fitzgerald," said the receptionist as he walked through the lobby. He picked up the key card waiting for him on the counter without stopping. They had been expecting him, but not for long. He had only booked a room a few hours before. "Welcome back, sir."

As the elevator climbed to the second floor, he craved a drink. He always did when he came here. The memories were powerful. Jett wasn't here for fun, though. He was here for a very specific reason. It would be his commitment alone that would keep him from the bar tonight. Standing alone in the elevator, he thought about exactly what had brought him here.

"Deal with her."

He was a man of his word and, more importantly, he was a man that always came prepared.

Chapter 45

January 2025 | Best Western Hotel
San Juan, Puerto Rico

The splash of cold water across Julie's face breathed life into her lungs. She did it a second and then a third time. She pressed her open palms onto her eyes after she flipped the water off. She hoped that when they opened again, the world would be a different place than it had been when she closed them. Julie pushed harder, exhaling through pursed lips. But when her lids finally opened, her reflection in the mirror stared back, exhausted and alone.

Julie was in her hotel room in a San Juan Best Western. Only a single lamp brought light into the room and the window shades were drawn. Though she was only a mile from the sandy beaches of the Atlantic Ocean, it looked exactly like the hundreds of hotel rooms she'd been in over the years. She tossed her suitcase on the floor and pulled off her uniform before falling into bed, feeling drained.

For the entirety of the flight from Tampa, Julie's eyes had never left the hydraulic pressure display. She had been on edge every second, but the pressure hadn't faltered. In fact, the plane had made it to the island without a hiccup. It had been a routine flight, really nothing exceptional about it, but that didn't mean the flight had been uneventful. From the moment the airplane's wheels had left the ground until the second they returned, every muscle in Julie's body had been taut. The strain had left her numb. When they had finally arrived on the island, she had never been so happy to check into a two-star hotel.

In bed, she rolled on her back and stared at the ceiling. She could hear someone's muffled footsteps walking down the hallway above and a baby crying in the room next door. She couldn't imagine being able to sleep. There was a potential leak in the hydraulic system on that airplane. Perhaps maintenance crews had patched it up, but it was only a matter of time before the problem resurfaced. Even though they had made it safely today, she'd have to co-pilot that plane back to Tampa tomorrow. She knew that the old system had flown for decades without an issue. It had persevered through years of service, but she also knew its expiration was nearing. Every flight was one closer to its finale.

Her troubles didn't stop there. Ryan had decided to extend an invitation in the air. *"Julie, let me take you out to dinner tonight."* The purr of the engines had been droning in the background and the Keys had been displayed in panoramic view. *"I'd love to catch up."* It was the single moment when Julie's attention had been distracted from the hydraulic pressure. She had been at a loss for words. Ryan had looked over to her, smiling, impervious to the way he made her feel. Julie had again sensed the embarrassment and shame creeping back.

"I'm getting married."

Now months later, Julie had found herself alone again with Ryan. Only this time the circumstances had been different, and her defenses were up. She had never wanted to see him again and thought she had made that clear. Instead, Ryan had pressed himself onto her again.

"I can't." Julie lied. She wanted to tell him that she loathed him, and that he was the type of person she had tried to protect herself from for all these years. She hated him for even being there; it was even worse that he was

asking more of her. She had wanted to tell him all of this, but she didn't. Instead, she had turned back to the hydraulic pressure. *"I am meeting another friend tonight for dinner."*

In the hotel room next door, the baby began to cry louder. She sat up in bed, squeezing her fists into balls. There was no time for her to be distracted by a personal history that shouldn't matter any more. She got to her feet, flipped her suitcase open and began to rummage in it. She needed to focus. More than anything, she needed to clear her mind. Ryan had taken enough from her and she needed to push him out. At the bottom of her suitcase, she found what she was looking for: her tennis shoes.

When things were tough, she always had this tool in her back pocket. Now, she needed it more than ever. She pulled on a pair of athletic shorts and tied her hair back. She grabbed her room key and left her phone on the nightstand. Out of the door, Julie shot down the hall. She passed through the elevator doors and headed towards the hotel lobby. She was energized, knowing some fresh air was what she needed. As she went out of the hotel door and under the awning, the warm island sun hit her face. For a second, she smiled.

Chapter 46

January 2025 | Best Western Hotel
San Juan, Puerto Rico

The hotel lobby always had a brew of slightly burnt coffee in the pot and the aroma hung in the air. It soaked into the walls and furniture, as it had for decades. In the lobby, receptionists bustled absently behind the counter and the occasional guest walked by, not noticing the man in the corner. Jett sipped slowly from a Styrofoam cup. He felt the gritty liquid slide down the back of this throat. It was hot and charred, but it gave just enough buzz. Sunglasses shaded his eyes under a baseball cap. Behind a newspaper, he sat quietly. He held it open, like a curtain, but he wasn't reading.

Jett Fitzgerald was watching the elevator. Closely.

He was dressed in shorts and a t-shirt, generic but adaptable. In a town of tourists, he would blend in wherever he went. Patiently, he waited. He knew she was here because he had studied her itinerary closely. He had access to the schedule for every pilot in the airline, and he had found hers with no more than a few clicks. She would come down, he knew it, and he would wait. He would sit here as long as he needed to.

"Deal with her."

Tonight, the Chief Pilot of Avionica Airlines was waiting for a meeting. It was unscheduled, but it was mandatory, nonetheless.

Chapter 47

January 2025 | Best Western Hotel
San Juan, Puerto Rico

"Can you take me to El Yunque?" Julie was standing at the backdoor of a yellow taxicab ready to hop in. Under the hotel awning, cars searched for parking around an airport shuttle unloading two families of four.

"Yes, ma'am," said the driver. She was an older woman, with tanned skin from a lifetime on the island. She gestured for her to get in and popped the car into drive. As Julie closed the taxi door, she was already happy to be away from that hotel room. The car accelerated west on highway 66 and out of town.

After so many layovers in Puerto Rico, Julie had become accustomed to the hotel. It was a quick walk to some decent food but, more importantly, it was only a ten-minute walk to the beach. After a few trips, she had had her fill of the beach and had explored further. El Yunque National Park was a scenic drive not far from the hotel and had quickly become her favorite spot on the island. Though the stunning beaches stirred Julie every trip she made, it was the park that she truly adored. On the eastern side of the island, it was one of only two rainforests within the United States. With stunning views from mountain peaks and winding ravines, walking the grounds felt like a scoop of heaven on earth. And if Julie was aching for anything after that claustrophobic flight today, it was for a wide-open space.

As they sped north on the six-lane highway, the early afternoon traffic was light. The driver navigated the familiar route with ease. Julie took a swig of her bottle of water and looked through the windshield. The vaulted mountain peaks cut through the horizon into vast wisps of puff clouds. Lush plant life carpeted the earth and danced in the light afternoon wind. In her athletic shorts and shirt, she was glad she had slathered her fair skin with sunscreen. When the cab turned off the parkway and into the reserve, she already felt lighter. Running the scenic trails and navigating the park would be exactly what she needed.

"You can pull off over here," she said. They were a mile back in the park when the cab pulled off the winding road. There was a small fenced in parking lot cut into the mountain, overlooking the valley below. In the distance, the blue Atlantic waves merged with the beaches at the edge of the island. From the mountainside, a waterfall echoed in the expanse and collected in a granite basin below. There was a shelter and benches, but it was empty.

"Can you come back in about an hour?" Julie paid the fare and passed the driver a few extra bills. Experience had taught her that a good tip brought the cab back and ensured she wouldn't get stranded. The driver smiled and thanked her, taking the money and assuring her she'd be back.

As the car pulled away, Julie looked over the valley. Rains high in the mountain nourished the lush expanse below, bringing the green spread all the way to the beaches ten miles away. She took in the view, breathing in the cleansing air and feeling the warm breeze kiss her skin. It was beautiful and the escape for which she had hoped.

Chapter 48

January 2025 | Best Western Hotel
San Juan, Puerto Rico

Jett Fitzgerald eyed Julie from across the hotel lobby. He had been waiting, unmoving in his post for hours, but she had finally appeared. In her athletic clothes, she emerged from the elevator and trotted past the reception desk. Watching her carefully, he didn't move so as not to draw attention to himself. She stepped outside through the automatic doors with a water bottle in her hand.

Jett's patience had paid off. Finally, she was in his sights. But his job was far from over.

He rolled up the newspaper and came to his feet. Not fast enough to draw eyes, but quick enough so not to lose her. Still hidden behind sunglasses and his red cap, he watched through the window. From under the awning, she waved down a cab. She spoke through the back window and finally jumped in. All the while, Jett was cautiously approaching the door. He observed her, making meticulous notes in his mind, but keeping his distance.

He would have his chance.

Sampers jumped into the back of the cab and slammed the door. As it waited to turn right out of the lot, Jett made his move. A black sedan sat waiting for him just beside the hotel awning and he slid into the driver seat. Keeping his eye on the taxi, he slid the key into the ignition and pulled it into drive.

Chapter 49

January 2025 | El Yunque National Park
San Juan, Puerto Rico

The trail was cut into the expanse of rainforest life. Julie's breathing quickened as her feet carried her higher into the mountain. Small streams brought rainwater toward the sea and massive leaves caught rays on the forest floor. She leaped over rocks and massive roots on the trail, while her tension eased with each step. The air was soggy with humidity, but she knew it would cool as she ascended.

As she ran, Julie smiled.

The reserve, enclosing 28,000 acres, was the oldest area of protected land in the western hemisphere. Well over hundreds of species thrived here; 20 of which were only seen in Puerto Rico. The remarkable diversity of life underpinned a thriving ecosystem unique to the land. Her favorite region in the park was the Dwarf Forest, where thick tree trunks rose from the earth and leaves covered nearly every millimeter of the floor.

As the afternoon sun began to fall to the west, she let her mind piece together everything she knew. Her sabbatical was ending in a few weeks and she needed something to show for it. If she didn't, everything that was important to her would be gone. She thought of Professor Jaxon, knowing he had understood all this decades earlier. Unfortunately, he hadn't been able to see it through to the end, which was what she needed to do.

A wooden bridge connected the two ends of a small ravine. A stream muttered below, and the trail began to ascend steeper. Still, she didn't slow down.

Science could explain the symptoms, and the reports made sense with the hypothesis, but it was all nothing without the evidence. What she ideally needed was objective proof that TCP was the culprit. The TCP swabs hidden in the bottom of her purse were the most valuable things that she possessed.

Beads of sweat dripped off her forehead and her ponytail was bouncing with each step. Her heart was beating harder and faster than it did on her usual run, but all the while, everything weighing on her was falling away. The views were stunning, but the trail was challenging. Most of her attention was on the next step, but her mind still wandered as she ran. Frank Brewer had told Julie to be careful. It was dangerous and Avionica was committed. But in spite of that, she continued forward. She was getting closer, but still needed more.

The trail came to a clearing and Julie slowed to a walk. She propped her hands on her hips, trying to expand the space between her ribs. After 30 minutes on the trail, she had made it to her destination. Nested along the green cliff overlooking the northern shoreline of the island, the Yokahu Tower was one of two vantage points in the park. Though it was often hidden in the clouds, it offered tremendous views of the valley below. It was a weekday afternoon, and the site was perfectly empty. In fact, the small parking lot beside the lookout tower didn't have a single car in it. The only noise Julie could hear was birdsong and a nearby creek. She was alone and, in the warmth of the island sun, it was absolutely perfect.

The structure was circular, constructed of grey brick, and it had a lookout platform high above the rainforest floor. The distance from the city brought clarity and she was glad to be alone at this moment. Feeling encouraged, she made for the door and began climbing the steps.

Chapter 50

January 2025 | El Yunque National Park
San Juan, Puerto Rico

The trail leveled into a clearing, where a circular tower overlooked the valley. It was tall, built of dull grey brick, with one open window. It looked abandoned and there were no visitors or cars in sight. Further back on the path, Jett Fitzgerald needed to stop to catch his breath. He had been bent over, propping his hands on his knees, but he still watched carefully. Sweat ran off his forehead and a blister was burning on his left foot. From a distance, he followed her. Getting himself up this mountain was arduous, but he was up to the task.

Sampers had left the cab near the entrance of the park. He had followed from behind but needed to ditch the car once she went into the forest. When she started up the trail, he was glad he had worn tennis shoes. He struggled to keep pace with her, but managed to not stay too far behind. He kept his distance so as not to be heard, but he never lost sight of her.

Now, the woman had stopped, and she was looking over the valley. Fifty yards from the tower, Jett watched her and worked to slow his breathing.

William Hoffman

He had sweat clear through his clothes and his blister was screaming, but he had made it. That's what counted.

When Sampers turned and started up the tower stairs, he smiled. He looked around a final time, not seeing a single soul. Not only had he climbed up an entire mountain, but he had waited patiently for this moment. Now, he would have the chance that he had been waiting for.

It was almost too easy.

Chapter 51

January 2025 | El Yunque National Park
San Juan, Puerto Rico

At the top of Yokahu Tower, Julie let herself be enveloped by a blanket of serenity. Resting her hands on the brick wall, she absorbed the 360-degree view of the island. She could see the buildings in San Juan and the white-capped waves beyond. Far off in the distance, a cruise ship sat on the horizon. In the port of San Juan, droves of tourists would soon disembark into the city. Behind her, the mountain peaks were hidden in the clouds. Of all the places she had enjoyed traveling to in her life, the peak of the Yokahu Tower was her favorite. A warm breeze blew through her hair and she let the worry exhale between her lips. Despite everything that had happened in the past few months – the stress, the heartache, the worry – her tensions seemed to be abating. From this spot, the problems of the world seemed smaller. She wished life could be as clear as it seemed from this spot. She closed her eyes, letting the fresh island air fill her lungs. Of all the places in the world to be, this was where Julie could find peace.

"Julie."

A man's voice was a violent assault on the silence. It came from behind her and forced her eyes open. She spun around reflexively. Pressing her back against the tower's outer wall, she held her breath. Who could possibly know she was here? Every muscle in her back squeezed. The tone was sharp but not loud. It was a tone that said, "I found you". She didn't think, she simply braced.

"Enjoying your run?" he said. The man was tall, wearing shorts and a sweaty t-shirt. Sunglasses hid his eyes, and a red baseball cap covered his grey hair. He stood between Julie and the stairs with his hands at his sides.

"Captain Fitzgerald?" Julie's pulse throbbed in her neck. Shock bubbled beneath her skin and she wanted to scream. Instead, she stood perfectly still.

"It's beautiful up here, isn't it?" he said. He took a single step towards her, staying between her and the exit. The tower was so quiet that Julie could hear each of his steps. "It's amazing the places we get to go." He looked over the valley, using the moment to take in the view. He had the situation by the throat, and he knew it.

"What are you doing here?" she asked. An urge to flee surged through her but there was no place to run to.

"I'm here for the same reason you are," he said, taking a step closer. His sunglasses shielded his eyes, but Julie could feel his stare. "Taking in the sights, I suppose you could say."

"Is everything okay?" she said, trying to hide the fear in her voice. She instinctively tried to take a step back, but the outer brick wall stopped her. Since coming to the airline, she had made it a point to never interact with the chief pilot. She had seen him once or twice, but she had tried to remain a faceless name in the crowd. Of course, she knew who he was, but she had hoped that it wasn't reciprocal.

"You tell me, Julie," he said, taking another step towards her. Their paths had crossed before in the Minneapolis ICU, but she could only hope he had forgotten. Now no more than six feet from him, her hands began to shake. Not only from fear, but also from the frantic adrenaline roaring through her veins.

"I'm afraid I don't know what you mean," she said. She swallowed heavily, immediately feeling small. Her voice was shaking but she tried to conceal it. What did he know? Like prey in the jaws of a hunter, she was defenseless.

"Now let me ask you a question." His powerful frame came nearer. As he approached, his voice grew quieter. "What are you doing here," he paused only a few feet away, "Professor Sampers?"

In a violent jolt, air was expelled from Julie's lungs. She tried to swallow again, but it was somewhere closer to a cough.

He knew.

"I'm sorry?" she asked, trying to buy time. She laughed, but it didn't ring true. Each second was long and merciless. Jett Fitzgerald remained absolutely still while Julie thought of Frank and his warnings.

"Don't play dumb," he said. Julie's mind was racing. "I know who you are."

She begged her body to move, but it wouldn't comply. She wanted to do something, anything but be trapped where she was. Julie knew about animal instinct. But in her entire life, she had never truly known how it felt. Now more than anything, she felt a visceral urge to escape.

"Why are you here, Julie?" he asked again. He inched forward.

"I'm here to fly, sir," she pleaded. "Really, I missed flying." Her throat was dry, and the words hardly came out. Her hands came up, nearly in surrender. It was a lie, that was for certain, but she could only hope that it would hold.

"I hope that's the truth, Julie," he said. With her back still against the tower wall, they were no more than two feet apart. "You're a good pilot." He took off his sunglasses and tucked them in his shirt. He squinted, reacting to the sun. "You're not cut out to be an academic," he said, "You're one of us."

Julie's breath came out in quick bursts. She searched for a way to get out, but there was none. "At least," he paused, "that better be why you're at Avionica."

Julie could feel the heat of his skin. She wanted to scream, but every cell in her body forced her to stay silent. She prayed for someone to stop this man from doing what he was about to do.

They were completely alone. No one would even hear her scream.

The wall behind her only came as high as her hip. It wasn't tall; she could feel the corner pressing into the small of her back. Beyond, the rocky floor of the forest was 75 feet below. Nothing would survive a fall from that height.

There was nowhere else to run.

Captain Fitzgerald took his forearm, muscular and powerful, and pulled it across his chest. He stepped towards her one final time, only inches from her body. In a swift motion, he pressed her towards the edge. In a split second, her feet were off the ground. Panic boomed while her hands searched frantically for something to grab on to. She let out a cry of fear. If he pushed any further, she would topple backward and below.

"And if I hear anything to the contrary," he pushed a little harder, "Or any word of this conversation," Julie's eyes widened as her arms searched wildly. "You will lose more than just a job."

"Please!" she cried out. Her weight was teetering on the edge of the wall. She grabbed his arm with both of hers, but he pushed back harder. She wondered if anyone would find her body on the earth below, but it wouldn't matter. It would be too late.

"I don't know who you think you are," he said in a near whisper, "Or what the hell you're doing," a tear fell silently from Julie's eye, "But I suggest you put some serious thought to it, because I am watching your every move."

Julie locked her arms around Jett's, but it was no use. If he pushed further, she would fall no matter what she did. She pictured the concrete below and the tourists who would later find her cold, lifeless body. She thought about Ron and her apartment in Grand Forks. She considered her life and the things she had still hoped to do. The students that loved her and the profession that meant everything. She had never thought this was how it would end, but she had no way to fight back.

Suddenly, relief came. In a single motion, he pulled his arm back and Julie fell to the ground. He moved back with caution. The tears were falling down her face. They were automatic and unwelcome. There was shock and there was fear, but mostly there was relief.

When she finally looked up, Jett Fitzgerald was at the top of the stairs. He looked back at her impassively, unmoved by the look in her eyes. He put his sunglasses back on and adjusted his hat. All the while, Julie didn't dare stand.

Before he turned and made his way down the stairs, the man said one final thing. It was simple, but Julie would never forget it. It wasn't angry, or even bitter. His voice was even, almost matter of fact. But when the words came, they cut Julie to the deepest corners of her body.

"You decide how this ends."

Chapter 52

January 2025 | San Juan International Airport
San Juan, Puerto Rico

After a sleepless night, Julie put on her uniform and headed to the airport early. So much had happened in the past 24 hours that she was in a trance, her mind distant. Before the rest of the crew had even arrived at the airport, Julie was already sitting alone in the cockpit.

It was still hard to believe. *"You decide how this ends."* Fear, panic and confusion were burning through her, but so were other feelings. She couldn't shake all that Frank Brewer had said, not only about the history of this story, but also his caution to proceed deeper. Any suspicions she had had before were both stronger and apparently justified. To think that it all could've ended with just a little more force, just one more inch, was overwhelming. The thought chilled her to her core. All she could do was not let herself think of what it could've meant for her. But of all the things that had kept her awake, one important fact had been affirmed beyond any remaining doubt.

There was credence to this story.

The encounter with Fitzgerald on the tower had vindicated this pursuit. They were worried so they sent someone. There was something to protect, so they were willing to risk more. She was scared, that was for certain, but she had also discovered a renewed sense of resolve. The problem was far bigger than Julie alone, but perhaps she had the tools to see it through. Most importantly, she needed to print the pictures of the maintenance records on her phone. That was her next step on the path forward. Unfortunately, there was one thing in her way. To get off this island and away from the man who had threatened her life, one variable still remained.

She would again have to fly this aircraft over the sea.

Julie's gut told her something wasn't right. She had tried to keep yesterday's flight on the ground but had ultimately submitted. While her suspicions were high, she had no definitive evidence this plane was unsafe and Avionica would fly regardless of the risk. Ryan had made that perfectly clear. The maintenance crew had said they were safe to fly, and Julie could only hope it was the truth. If their pre-flight checklists showed no issue, Julie would have to take this plane back to Tampa loaded with fuel, mail and people.

"Good morning, Julie," said Ryan. He stepped through the cockpit door and started taking off his blazer. "I didn't see you at the hotel breakfast this morning."

Instead of taking the crew shuttle from the hotel, Julie had decided to take a cab. Not only had she needed some space to think, but she needed space from Ryan.

"Wanted to get an early start," said Julie, not looking back.

The passengers boarded, the luggage was stowed, and the fuel tanks were filled. As Julie had feared, the pre-flight checks were unrevealing. The plane was pushed back from the gate with 140 people aboard. Ryan started the engines and Julie verified their route. Once again, she constantly kept her eye on the hydraulic pressure reading. It was normal, at least for the moment. The sealed system was generating enough force to work the flaps, landing gear and flight controls. She kept watching, almost wishing it to falter. If the hydraulic pressure dropped before take-off, it would be a relief. They would return to the gate and Julie, along with all of those onboard, would walk away unscathed. But if it dropped in the air, the situation would be entirely different. As the Avionica airliner turned off the taxiway at the end of the runway, she wasn't reassured by the normal pressure reading. She knew that old, tired seals could give way in an instant.

At the head of the runway, they received their departure clearance. The final check list was completed while Julie's heart raced.

"Are you ready to go, Julie?" asked Ryan.

Julie looked at the hydraulic pressure reading one final time. "I guess so," she said.

Ryan released the brakes and pushed the controls forward. The engines came alive, and the airplane rumbled ahead. As the main gear of the A320 pulled off the runway, Julie tried to let herself breathe. Everything she had worked so hard for had been for the right reason. People wanted to stop her, but she persisted. There were secrets that the world needed to know. The plane lifted off the runway and Julie let a single breath fill her lungs. As the airliner climbed, the landing gear retracted. The world grew smaller, and the ocean extended beneath them. The dynamic hue of blues and greens extended with the ocean into the distant horizon, where it met the cloudless sky.

"Shit," Ryan said.

An alarm chimed and Julie held her breath. Dread filled her chest because she knew exactly what was about to happen. On the panel, two warning lights began to blink ominously. Like Julie's sudden fear, the bell was persistent and strong. A chilling message populated on the panel display.

HYD Y RSVR LO LVL

The block letters read as she feared. Julie watched the symphony in stunned dismay.

"Looks like the problem is in the yellow reservoir," said Ryan. His eyes were combing over the panel. "The PTU just turned on."

"Let's run the checklist?" Julie asked. She was already reaching for the manual as she spoke. She let her training take over, but she couldn't ignore the fear surging through her. In an instant, the world had started crumbling down. What she had feared had become reality.

"Make sure the circuit is isolated," said Ryan. He was studying the controls. "Turn off the PTU and isolate the yellow side." There was a hint of fear in his voice. "I think we're leaking hydraulic fluid to the yellow system." Julie's training made her fingers glide across the panel in a predetermined sequence. She worked quickly and decisively.

"Warning still illuminated," she said after resetting the system. "Pressure is below 500 PSI." Fighting to suppress her nerves, Julie's eyes were wide. "Four thousand feet," she called out. She had trained for emergencies countless times, but she knew that whatever happened next depended on far more than her experience alone. "Climbing at two hundred and thirty-four knots."

"Shit, okay," Ryan's voice cracked. "Let's run the checklist." Without needing to say a word, they both knew how real the danger was. The hydraulic system was a series of mechanical tubes that worked key aircraft systems. Most importantly, it worked the control surfaces on the wing. Julie opened the manual just as the phone began to ring. It went to the passenger cabin and a flight attendant would be on the other end of the line.

"Julie, you have controls and radios," said Ryan. During an emergency, it was often practice for the first officer to fly the airplane so the captain could troubleshoot.

"I have controls," Julie responded. She passed the book to her left while her heart throbbed beneath her breastbone. She placed her right hand on the control stick and her left on the throttles.

"This is the captain," Ryan said into the cabin phone. The confident ease Julie had always known had faded from his voice. There was a long pause and Julie's stomach squeezed. Only moments after departure, a call from a flight attendant could only mean a few things. While the alarm kept cycling, Julie thought of all the possibilities. It was hard to believe she had found herself in the exact predicament she had been trying so hard to prevent.

"Got it." Ryan said sharply. He hung up the phone on the central console and turned his attention back to the checklist. The 135-page manual served as a pilot's guide through an emergency, and they knew it well. Ryan paged through the index while Julie focused on the controls.

"Yellow reservoir low pressure," said Ryan, turning back to the displays. The aircraft had three hydraulic circuits: green, blue and yellow. Each generated enough pressure to operate different components of the aircraft. In an emergency, a reservoir could be isolated, and pressure adjusted by an override system. The issue was that the override system only worked if there was sufficient hydraulic fluid.

"What is our plan, Ryan?" asked Julie, looking left. She waited for direction, but he just paged urgently through the manual. "Should I keep climbing?"

"Just hold on!" Ryan shot back and Julie flinched. He flipped pages and skimmed quickly while mumbling something to himself. Seconds were ticking by and Julie sensed he was buying time to think. "We'd better turn back to the field," he finally said.

"Do you want to declare an emergency?" asked Julie. A third panel light began to flash, and the alarm wailed. Julie eyed the display again, seeing the pressure drop further. There wouldn't be much time. Ryan kept flipping through the manual while the island grew further behind them. "And what is going on in the cabin?"

"Good idea." Ryan looked up, seeming to waver as he thought. "Okay, I'll declare an emergency."

"Ryan," Julie cut, not letting her eyes leave the controls. "What was that call about?"

He hesitated. A look of alarm had now completely replaced his usual demeanor. "It was the back," said Ryan distractedly. He closed the manual and started paging from the beginning again. "There's a little fog in the cabin."

Ryan contacted San Juan Tower and explained their situation. They declared an emergency and were vectored back to the field. By now, they had been in the air no longer than three minutes.

"Roger, turn right heading two six zero for Avionica 144," replied Julie over the radio.

But as she said the final word to the controller, something changed. It wasn't clear, but, like an aura or a premonition, Julie could feel it approaching with violent speed. It was elusive, but powerful. Whatever it was, Julie knew it was coming and she couldn't stop it.

Without warning, a violent pain stabbed through her skull. It was sharp, like a hot knife stabbing behind her orbits. The force pushed her back in her seat and she had to close her eyes. The pain was more than she had ever known. Then there was the spinning, a force more powerful than she had ever thought possible. The sensation was staggering, like she was somersaulting. When she finally opened her eyes, the cockpit was hazy and unfocused.

"Julie?" said Ryan. There was fear in his voice.

The pain fell over her like tsunami waves. She blinked, but nothing would come into focus. Then, her hand began to tingle. First it was the left, but then it hit the right side too. Millions of needles seemed to stabbing progressively deeper into her skin. It was happening so quickly, so dramatically, that Julie could hardly think.

"Julie are you okay?" he asked again.

The airplane continued to bank but the space around her grew more distant. Almost like a dream, it felt like she was seeing the world through someone else's eyes. Despite the rapidly changing visual cues, she fought to remain focused.

And then without warning, she began to cough. The reflex was powerful and she could focus on nothing else. Her throat felt tight as she gasped for air. But before she realized what was happening, Ryan began to cough too. Reality felt distant and her world was clouding over. The sounds of the engines grew more remote, and gravity pulled her deeper into her seat. She heard her name, but the words were becoming progressively distant.

Moments before she drifted away to a place where the world was dark and her mind was free, she felt pressure on her face. There was hissing and an odor. It was sharp and inorganic, like rubber or metal.

Julie could no longer move. The air tasted chemical, and it made her saliva pool. Was this the end? Darkness was collecting around her, pulling her closer into a womb. No matter how hard she fought it, she would lose. The urge to cough was easing, but the darkness was complete. She began to feel warmer, and the tingling wasn't so uncomfortable. It covered her whole body, but it didn't hurt. She heard the engines and her name being called but it was even further away. Everything was calm because she wasn't in control. Then in an instant, her world went black.

Chapter 53

January 2025 | San Juan International Airport
San Juan, Puerto Rico

When Julie resurfaced, the world was quieter. Her head was throbbing, and the light made her eyes burn. She squinted and leaned forward into her shoulder harness. Gobs of saliva were pooled in her mouth and dripping onto her shirt. She wiped her chin with the back of her hand. She let her head fall back onto the seat while she pulled the world into focus. An oxygen mask was pressed over her face. It hissed as the air was pushed into her nose and mouth.

"It's going to be okay ma'am," said a man behind her. He reached over her shoulder and began unfastening her harness. "We're going to take you to the hospital."

The world was slowly returning but the reality was strange. Julie tried to sit up, but she was weak and unsteady. Her eyes searched around, trying to get oriented, but everything was out of focus. She was dizzy and the movement made the spin faster. The man behind her unlatched her mask and pulled it off her face. Her head ached, made worse by the urge to cough. There was an eerie silence, which made her fear spike.

Without warning, two people then hoisted Julie from her seat. She tried to fight it, extending her legs as if to stand, but she nearly fell.

"Where…" her voice was raspy, and she coughed. "Where's Ryan?" she finally said.

"I'm right here," said Ryan. He was standing in the galley watching through the cockpit door. Beyond him, lines of people were hastily disembarking through exits in both the front and back of the plane. Julie stumbled to take a step forward. "You're going to be okay, Julie." There was worry in his voice. "The fire fighters are going to take you to the hospital."

The silence was deafening. The roar of the engines had ceased, and the airplane was still. Through the cockpit windshield, Julie could see they had stopped on the runway. The engines were off, and the cockpit was dark. She tried to recall everything that had happened, but the thoughts were distant and hazy. She remembered the call from the cabin and the turn towards the field. An emergency had been declared, and the pressure was low. Then only the headache, the coughing and the darkness.

"What…" Julie's voice was dry. The fire fighters struggled to get her through the cockpit door. "What happened?" Julie managed. There were sirens outside of the plane and yellow emergency slides deployed from the doors. It was an evacuation.

"Just try to relax, ma'am," said the fire fighter. "You were unconscious." Two of them were supporting her entire weight.

"Wait, please," she started. She was starting to get her bearings. They finally carried her out of the cockpit and towards the door. "Just wait a second, please." The pain in her head made speaking almost unbearable.

"It's all okay, Julie," started Ryan. He touched her shoulder. "I got us back on the runway."

"My bag," said Julie, struggling against the rescuers. She coughed again and swallowed. "Ryan, please! My bag."

"Stay calm and exit in an orderly fashion." A flight attendant was repeating over the public address system. Her tone was at odds with the scene. In the cabin, the last few fearful passengers were filling the aisles and hurrying out of the exits. Some were coughing while some helped others to the doors.

"I'm here, Julie." At the boarding door, Ryan came to Julie's side. "I'm right here."

"There's a box in the bottom of my bag, Ryan," Julie struggled. Her legs were so weak that she was nearing hanging from the firemen's arms. Around them, passengers shuffled to the exits holding clothing and napkins over their faces. "Behind the seat," she managed.

"Ma'am, please," interrupted the fire fighter. He was pushing her forward. "We need to get you to a hospital."

"Ryan, *please!*" Julie cried. The plea in her voice made the fire fighter pause. The call was desperate, but more important than he could possibly know.

Ryan was frazzled but he complied. He reappeared from the cockpit with the grey box in his hand. It was no bigger than a dollar bill. She was clumsy and slow, but she eventually managed it open. Inside, 12 TCP saliva swabs, individually wrapped, stood ready.

"Swab the inside of your mouth," she told him. Julie nearly buckled again at the knees again, but the fire fighter caught her. She carefully unwrapped one for herself and started scrapping inside her cheek.

"Ma'am, please," urged the fire fighter. "We need to go." He spoke sternly but Julie didn't back down.

"What is this?" asked Ryan. He studied it, looking wary.

"Just do it, Ryan," Julie pleaded. She didn't have the strength to explain anything now. Her vision was clearing but the headache still pervaded. She was weak, but the spinning was mercifully easing. Without any more questions, Ryan complied. He scraped the inside of his cheeks and then studied it carefully.

"It's turning blue," Ryan said. Near the handle, a square indicator changed color.

Julie tried to bring her own into focus. After she swabbed, she held it close to her eyes and watched the square closely. Her vision was blurred, but she could see the result. Hers also turned blue.

"That's enough," commanded the firefighter again. "It's time to go." The two pulled Julie to the door and she was too weak to protest.

"What are these, Julie?" Ryan followed behind them, holding his test in hand. He was desperate, made so by all that he had just endured.

"Take the rest of the swabs," called Julie over her shoulder. She yelled with all the energy she had left. "Find other passengers with symptoms and have them do the same thing." She desperately tried to turn back towards Ryan, but the fire fighters overpowered her. There were stairs at the main door, and they carried her down.

"What do these mean?" called Ryan, who was following behind them. At the bottom of the stairs, Julie was laid on a stretcher behind an ambulance. They opened the doors to load her inside.

"Just do this for me, Ryan," she called back. She surrendered and finally fell onto the stretcher. Beyond the pain, she was defeated with exhaustion. But before they closed the ambulance door, she had one more thing she had to say.

"You'll understand soon."

Intrepid Pursuit

Part 3

Chapter 54

May 2025 | University of North Dakota
Grand Forks, North Dakota

"On a cloudy morning in May 1927, a single engine aircraft taxied through a muddy field a few miles from Long Island, New York. Charles Lindbergh sat on a wicker chair ready to make history." Professor Julie Sampers paced in front of her captivated audience. The springtime air was making way for summer, and more flowers were soon to bloom. On the western edge of campus, the lecture hall was full and completely silent. One hundred of North Dakota's future aviators sat in the amphitheater entirely captivated by their instructor.

"After over 3,000 miles of looming storms, icing conditions, and staggering fatigue, he became the first person in history to fly across the Atlantic Ocean." Students from across the country sat with their books closed and eyes forward. Some leaned back in their chairs, while others were forward paying close attention. "In thirty-three and a half hours, he forever changed aviation."

Julie sensed she held the attention of the entire room. She paused with emphasis, holding their emotions in her hand. There were few things she loved more than aviation, but teaching was one of them. It was a privilege for which she lived.

"In a time when the world's final frontier was the sky, men and women just like you stepped forward to discover what lies beyond. Their bravery and passion created aviation as we know it." Her eyes surveyed the class, connecting with many. "When you leave these halls, you too will be a member in the long line of aviation's history." She paused and smiled. At the center of the room, she stood with her feet together and hands interlaced. "Congratulations on your studies and have a wonderful summer."

The room erupted in applause. As the hall began to clear, a twinge of emotion pulled at her eyes, a bitter sweetness she always felt at the end of an academic year.

"An impressive performance as always, Julie," said a familiar voice. The room had emptied, and she was gathering her things. At the top of the steps, a round man stood at the railing looking down. His smile was broad, and his warmth filled the room. "You certainly didn't lose the ability to grab their imagination while you were gone."

"Thanks Ron." Julie smiled. She put the rest of her notes in her bag and brought the strap over her shoulder. "It feels so good to be back."

"You were clearly missed," he said. He was coming down the stairs slowly, pressing his weight on the railing. "It's hard to believe you've already been back for a month. The department wasn't the same without you."

Julie blushed. She was grateful to the faculty for letting her return and finish the year. Though it had taken some time to fully recover from what had happened in San Juan, she was again thriving in the work she loved. "I'm happy to be back," she said, taking a step towards him. "I just hope I'll be able to stay."

At the bottom of the stairs, he smiled. "You and I both," he said. With his retirement looming, this year would be his last. Julie could sense the hint of nostalgia was not hers alone. "So, the million-dollar question," he started. "How is the paper coming?"

When Julie wasn't teaching her classes, she was endlessly working. At home, in her office, and even in the library, she was writing and rewriting day and night. She compiled the data, generating a case that would be impossible to refute. She had kept Cathy Anderson nameless, but had included her story along the maintenance logs. She had analyzed the problem from every angle, squaring every question she anticipated, and triple checking the facts. When it was done, it was airtight. The claim was a radical one, but Julie was ready to unveil it to the world.

On the plane that day, her saliva swab had turned blue. Importantly, so had the swabs of other passengers. As Julie had been riding to the hospital, Ryan had swabbed the others and found the same results. Now back at UND, Julie had incorporated Professor Jaxon's work into the manuscript, giving full credit for his role. She used his data to show that the swabs undeniably confirmed exposure to the toxin. TCP was the culprit for Aerotoxic Syndrome and now she had proof. When the manuscript was finally published, it would be the first study detailing the exact events of an Aerotoxic Syndrome fuming event. It would be historic, but most importantly, it would bring attention to this cause. No one could look away any longer. Certainly, the data was imperfect, and the swabs were not enough, but it would finally generate the momentum needed to bring about true change.

"I finished it." She smiled, nervous but full of excitement. "And they've already accepted it!" After months with so much on the line, she could hardly believe it herself. She was ready to publish a paper that would rock the industry. It wouldn't be in the depths of some academic journal either. The reach would be far broader. When she had initially sent the brief to the editor, Julie hadn't been optimistic. The *New York Times* wouldn't be interested, she was certain of it. She had initially resisted sending it, but Ron had encouraged her. As with every step of her career, Ron had guided her forward. But on the day when Julie was notified of the editor's decision, she had hardly been able to believe it. They would publish it as soon as it was received.

"You should be really proud of yourself, Julie," said Ron. Julie struggled to find the words to express the depth of her gratitude, but she sensed he knew. This was about more than a job. Even if her teaching contract wasn't renewed at the end of the year, Julie would know she had given it her all and that Ron had been her foundation every step of the way. Standing in the classroom where they had shaped the lives of hundreds of young pilots, two aviators from different generations tried to comprehend something bigger than they could put into words. She took a step forward and put her arms around him.

"No matter what happens, Julie," he said as he returned her embrace. "You've made a difference in this world."

Chapter 55

May 2025 | University of North Dakota
Grand Forks, North Dakota

Julie walked the hallway of John D. Odegard Hall on the west end of campus smiling. To the left and up the stairs from her classroom, she nearly floated to her office. After everything, it seemed her efforts would soon pay off.

When this paper was published, it was hard to know what would happen. Though Julie knew it was something that needed to be released, she wasn't naive about the waves it would generate. The FAA and airlines would be questioned. There would be progress, but there would also be pain. It would be expensive, and there would be trials. With any great stride, there was sacrifice and Julie could only hope the right people would pay. Whatever happened, she hoped the deceptions would be rectified and the industry would change for the better. Along the way, of course, she also hoped she would keep her job.

When Julie had woken up in the hospital bed in Puerto Rico, there had been a company representative at her bedside. He had said he was a lawyer but offered little else. He lingered, watching her closely, but Julie had been too disoriented to say anything anyway. When he finally left, there had been an envelope on the nightstand that a nurse had read aloud to her.

```
Dear Valued Employee,

We regret that you have experienced an unfortunate
event. You are not to make any statements to a
member of the press or speak of the event unless
otherwise directed. If you do not abide by this
direction, legal charges to the highest possible
extent will be pursued.

              Respectfully,

              Avionica Airlines Management Team
```

Over the days that followed, Julie had slowly recovered. The dizziness had ebbed, but the cloudiness had lingered. The company had made a brief statement about the event, but the news had been vague. They called it a mechanical failure, taking much of the script from Minneapolis, and the coverage was brief. The NTSB launched an investigation and interviewed Julie. Two investigators saw her in the hospital, taking detailed notes of her statement. She told them about the hydraulic pressure, the sudden headache and cough. She described the call from the cabin and the smoke. She hid nothing, detailing the maintenance records and her concern about Aerotoxic Syndrome. She had even offered to give them the TCP saliva swabs but, to her surprise, they had not been interested. In fact, they had said very little. They thanked her for her time, and then left.

Julie had flown back to Tampa and then resigned from the airline. She had mailed a letter, leaving the return address blank, and cited medical reasons for her departure. She had recovered in her Grand Forks apartment before returning from her sabbatical. When the NTSB had published their report, Julie had been floored. They labeled it a mechanical error and called for no change. She had been stunned and furious, but it had only fueled her need to publish what she had found.

Intrepid Pursuit

On the third floor of Odegard Hall, she checked her mailbox. It was the last day of the academic year and the office was quiet. Most were preparing for a two-month vacation, while others for a summer term. She paged through the junk mail and recycled most of it. She smiled at some faculty members and spoke briefly to others. She kept it light, but she was uneasy. Though the exchanges were bright, it was still not certain whether she would be returning in the fall and it seemed that no one dared to ask her.

At her office, she put the key in her door. But when she turned the lock, she realized something was off. The door was already unlocked. When she opened it, her bag nearly fell to the floor.

"Good afternoon, professor." A tall man, muscular in build, sat behind her desk. He was occupying her chair with his feet propped up and hands interlaced behind his head. "I was going to wait for your office hours," said Avionica Airlines owner Bruce Luxton drolly. He brought his legs down and leaned forward onto the desk. "But I simply couldn't wait."

"What are you doing here?" asked Julie breathlessly. Feeling vulnerable, her calm had suddenly evaporated. He got to his feet, guided her in and closed the door behind her. She wanted anything but to be in this room, but she felt her body limply comply. She took the seat opposite her desk.

"This is a rather sad office if I say so myself," he said. He sat behind her desk again. "But academia is different from industry, I suppose."

"What do you want?" she said. Julie tried to sound strong but felt oppressed under his presence. They had never met, but he had needed no introduction. An image of the El Yunque lookout tower surged into her mind.

"I'm here to talk," he said. He crossed his legs, leaning back assuredly. "I'm here to discuss your research."

Julie's stomach sank. She wanted to deny it, but no words would come.

"I hear you have an interest in our aircraft maintenance," he said. "So..." he paused. Amused, he opened up his hands and smiled. "Let's talk." He was a man who was used to negotiation and savored having the upper hand. "My airline hasn't done anything illegal," he started. "You can get the most expensive lawyers you want because it's the truth." Julie thought about the manuscript on her computer. It was on her desk, but he was sitting in her way. "I made my airline the most profitable in the country," he continued, "without breaking the law." He leaned forward and looked at her squarely. "Saying anything other than that would be libel."

"Why are you here, Mr. Luxton?" she asked flatly. "I'm sure you're not here to simply tell me you did nothing wrong."

The owner looked closely at her, unmoved by her challenge. Like a chess player, he was studying the board and looking several moves ahead.

"Professor Sampers," his eyes narrowed. "I built one of the most successful airlines in history," he paused. "I pay almost 30,000 employees among the highest wages in the industry." The dark centers of his pupils pressed into her, studying her carefully. "I work tirelessly to keep it working at its highest efficiency. I expect my employees to do the same."

"Mr. Luxton, there is no question your company is profitable," Julie said.

"You should know our company rests in a delicate balance," he interrupted. Julie remained unmoved in her seat. "And any displacement from that state will cause it to break apart."

"I understand, but..." she started, but he spoke over her.

"I know you plan to publish something," he said. He was serious but unrushed. "It will destroy the company and put 30,000 people out of work. That is 30,000 families that will not be fed, thousands of bills that will go unpaid, and many people that will lose their livelihood." He leaned back again in his chair. Julie didn't move. She could feel her cheeks reddening, surprised and taken off guard.

"And this will all be because of you, Julie," he pressed. His tone again grew sharper. He waited on cue to let the words sink in. "You're about to change thousands of lives in a horrendous way."

"I didn't do anything wrong!" she cut. The sudden shift of blame stung. "I'm simply telling the truth."

"It all depends on you, Julie." He smiled, visibly pleased with her defense. It only made it worse that she knew he was manipulating her to feel this way. It was exactly what he wanted. There was a long pause while he waited for her to be exactly where he wanted her. "I'm prepared to offer you a job," he said. He was ready for a reaction, but Julie tried not to give him one. "You will be the new Avionica Airlines Director of Safety," he said. He leaned forward, narrowing his focus. "You will oversee flight operations starting immediately." He pulled a card out of his suit jacket with a number on it so large that Julie had to count the zeroes. "This will be your salary."

Julie's mouth fell open.

"We will make the fixes you direct." His back straightened, seeing he was making ground. "Your concerns will remain internal, but the corrections will be made immediately." He smiled, relishing her disbelief. "You will be a leader at Avionica and be a part of our future."

"Safety Director?" Julie was dazed. Given that amount of money, her options would grow exponentially. Maybe she could really fix this airline and do some good. Her life would change in many ways and maybe she could change the lives of others too. But to take this job and stay silent seemed impossible. In many ways, she felt a duty to publish her paper, but it was hard to imagine the thought of contributing to the loss of 30,000 jobs. "How would I know you'd make the changes I've suggested?" she asked. "These are real people at risk."

"Far more people will be hurt if you don't make the right decision here, Julie," said the owner. He got to his feet and fastened the top button of his blazer. At the door, he looked back at her one final time. He held the knob in his hand, moments before stepping out of Julie's office and towards his private jet at Grand Forks International Airport. Once aboard, it would fly south towards a yacht waiting for him in the Caribbean. Julie wanted more time, she had more questions and needed to better understand. Instead, she was quiet.

"You have one day to decide, professor," he said. "But I suspect you'll make the right choice."

Part 4

Chapter 56

August 2025 | Downtown
St. Paul, Minnesota

A warm yellow hue spilled from lights hanging from the arched ceiling and fell across the oak wooden floors. Red bricks, worn from age, were stacked on the far wall between eight bay windows displaying the metropolitan city street beyond. An easy tune in 4/4 time played from the stand-up bass and piano while some 50 people chatted in casual summer attire. The old warehouse was tucked along Vandalia Street, not far from the historic mansions on Summit Avenue. Clusters of locals chatted easily with a drink in hand, about the Minnesota Twins' recent win against the Milwaukee Brewers.

Julie stood at the center of the room in a dress she'd bought just for the occasion. It was sky blue, pulled into her curves and cut at her knee. Her trim physique was snug in the cotton and her black heels clicked as she walked. With a glass of white wine in hand, she smiled at some people and spoke briefly with others, but she had come to this occasion by herself. The evening sun was falling over the horizon, and the St. Paul city streets were beginning to fill with locals out on the town. At the venue, dinner would be served within the hour but the open cocktail bar was more popular at the moment.

Julie looked around the room, her feet together and her stemmed glass in hand. She was less nervous than she had thought she would be. Today was a big day, one that had been on her mind for some time, but she felt calm. She had considered not coming, making some excuse, but had decided against it. She was a strong person, made even more so by the past few months, and this would be testimony to it. It was the beginning of August and she had become accustomed to her summer routine of late mornings, afternoons reading, and long walks around the city. In fact, after everything that had happened, this was the only event on her entire summer calendar.

"Julie," she heard a familiar voice. She turned, immediately seeing a face she knew well. He was wearing a shiny black tuxedo. "I'm so glad you came." He smiled.

"Of course, Ryan. I wouldn't have missed it." Since the ceremony, he had been fielding guests with his beautiful, glowing bride. Julie had waited patiently, watching from a distance. She saw him today in a way she had not before. The feelings were still complicated, and there was still much that hadn't been said, but it seemed unimportant now. Despite everything that had driven them apart, what had happened on that plane had brought them together in a new way. Not in friendship, but in the way that people come together after facing something that truly changes the course of their lives. Their stories would part, Julie would be sure of it, but she had come here today as a thank you. For what he had done, Julie was grateful. Without Ryan using the TCP swabs, Julie could not have finished this expedition. Everything else was behind them and Julie was only interested in looking forward.

"And congratulations," Julie smiled and blushed. "It was a beautiful wedding."

"I'm so sorry for what happened, Julie," said Ryan. True sorrow suddenly made its presence felt but Julie didn't let herself be moved under its weight. "It's just not fair."

Julie looked down. "I guess it is for the best." The wound was still new, and the reminder burned.

"So, what's next for you?" Ryan asked. The band's tune ended with a swipe of the high-hat and polite applause followed. Conversation grew and laughter peppered the air. The question was one Julie had been stewing on for weeks. After packing up her apartment in Grand Forks, she had thought about adventures somewhere new. It was bitter-sweet, far harder than that at times, but it was the truth. Where the future would take her was not clear yet, but North Dakota was no longer her home.

"I'll have to see," Julie smiled, hiding her true heartache. "I rented a small cottage on the beach for a while." She spun the stem of her wine glass in her hand. "Puerto Rico for now and then only the future will tell."

"What you did was really amazing, Julie," said Ryan. Another guest offered the groom congratulations and Ryan gave thanks over his shoulder. There were smiles and embraces. It was a happy time, one for celebration, but Julie had never felt more alone. The feeling wasn't loneliness or solitude, it was something different. Standing at the wedding of the man she had once loved, she felt a sense of true independence. With her shoulders back and breathing easily, she felt liberation. "I just cannot believe they let you go because you didn't publish the manuscript."

It hadn't explicitly been said but Ron had gently explained it to her. Under the guise of tightening budgets and research priorities, Professor Julie Sampers' paid contract was not renewed. With the help of Ron's advocacy, Julie was asked if she would stay on as a voluntary, unpaid faculty member. She had declined. She was young, turning 31 the following week, and needed to move on.

"I think it'll all work out for the best," she said. A group by the bar suddenly roared in laughter and a couple danced slowly past the band. The summer evening was becoming night and the world felt calm. The loss resounded in Julie's heart but so did a sense of growing momentum.

"How are things at Avionica?" Julie asked. She brought the cool oaky flavors of the Bordeaux to her lips and let them swirl between her teeth.

"They gave me two weeks off, if you can believe it," said Ryan. Julie could feel the group of people behind her waiting for their turn, and sensed their time together was drawing to an end. "I'm not sure if you heard," added Ryan. "They grounded the entire Avionica fleet." He smiled knowingly, leaving much more unsaid. "They're doing a major overhaul."

"An overhaul?" Julie said. "It's about time." She tried not to give too much away, but this was news to her. After she had submitted her research to them, she had not heard anything from the FAA. She had assumed that sending something so significant would at least bring a letter of acknowledgment. Instead, there had only been silence. She had been worrying it might have fallen into a pit at a federal office building in Washington, DC.

"They are scheduling two weeks of maintenance for every Airbus in the fleet," said Ryan. "Something urgent came from the FAA and they're doing major repairs." Julie stood perfectly still. "And they're replacing the hydraulic systems on our oldest airplanes." Ryan smiled and Julie held her breath. "I guess there was something that had forced their hand."

The afternoon Bruce Luxton had come to her office had changed everything. For hours, Julie had anguished over her decision. Submitting the manuscript to the *New York Times* would compel an industry to grow for the safety of the millions who rely on it. It would sustain her tenure at the university and perhaps even carve her name into history. It could change so much and generate personal gain. But putting this knowledge into the world through the media could collapse an airline, put tens of thousands of people out of work, and cast doubt on an industry where the margins were thin. Luxton's offer had briefly seemed like a possibility. She had wondered if she could bring about the change that was needed while sealing her professional future. The payoff would be massive in many senses. But the more Julie had considered it, the more it became clear she couldn't do it. It would be selling out, letting an industry use money to cheat accountability. And though she could perhaps bring change to

Avionica, if his promises of cooperation weren't just a bluff, it would leave other airlines unchecked.

"So, what did you actually do with that paper you were working on?" asked Ryan. The line was lengthening, and the next couple was eagerly waiting to speak to the groom. "About Aerotoxic Syndrome," he continued. "And the swabs we got that day."

Julie smiled. "I gave it all away," she said. "I submitted it all in an anonymous safety complaint to the FAA." She had given them everything: Professor Jaxon's data, the research, and the TCP saliva swabs. She had given them the details, the pictures and all the facts. The FAA had the proof of Aerotoxic Syndrome and the next move was theirs. It hadn't been perfect, but it had seemed like a natural end. Julie had done her part, and now they would have to take it from there. "I hadn't heard anything for weeks and I had assumed it was lost or ignored."

On the first day of the summer vacation, Julie had called Bruce Luxton. She had declined the job but said she would not publish the results. She had kept it brief, not sharing her reasons, and he had agreed. *"You've made the right decision, Julie,"* Luxton had said. *"Thousands of people will keep their jobs because of this."* One week later, a discreet envelope had come to her apartment by mail. There was no note, only a check. In the upper left corner, the company seal of Avionica Airlines was inscribed in black. It was written out to Professor Julie Sampers for an amount far beyond her yearly salary at the university. Little else needed to be said because the memo line said it all.

```
For the future of my airline.
```

"Julie," Ryan took a step forward. "There's more. The FAA put out a statement requiring all Airbus A320s to have their hydraulic systems replaced." He smiled. "I don't think it was a coincidence." Julie didn't know what to say. She looked away, working to fight back a tear. "So much has changed at Avionica since you've left," continued Ryan. "It turns out Luxton is being investigated for money laundering and is looking for someone to buy the airline." He laughed. "Lawyers are expensive I guess."

"Are you serious?" Julie said. It had only been a few weeks earlier that she had talked to him.

"It's not just him," Ryan said. "The whole place seems to be clearing out. Michael Burben suddenly resigned too." He smirked. "Most people seem to think he's running from something."

"And Jett Fitzgerald?" Julie asked. Too often she replayed those moments on the San Juan tower in her mind. She would never forget the cold look of focus in his eyes.

"Funny you ask," said Ryan. The group behind him was growing inpatient and the crowd by the bar was becoming louder. "He's taking a leave of absence now that he's under investigation." Julie remained still. "The police used his cell phone to place him in the park the day Frank Brewer died. People at the airline cannot stop talking about it."

Under the warm yellow lights, Julie placed her unfinished glass of wine on an empty table. A weight had been pulled from her shoulders and, for the first time in months, Julie breathed easy. Outside, the summer breeze blew calmly through the St. Paul city streets and over the slowly passing waters of the Mississippi River.

In their final moments together, Julie put her hand out to Ryan. Their journey together was coming to a close and her future remained uncertain, but she was ready to move ahead towards whatever was in store. Ryan smiled, but instead of shaking her hand, he wrapped his arms around her. "Good luck, Julie," he said. "You've really done something amazing."

The music was stopped, and someone invited the guests to their tables over the mic. Ryan was quickly ushered to the front, where his groomsmen and family were waiting. A three-course meal was soon to be served and the wine was only beginning. The room was flushed with bliss and the sense of potential that a wedding brings. There was laughter and joy but, most importantly, there was hope.

William Hoffman

As the guests came forward, Julie hung back. She took her time, mindful of each step. Before she opened the door at the back of the hall, she looked back one final time at Ryan. Their paths had crossed in an unusual way, but their connection would be forever sealed by everything that happened over the last year. Even though their paths would not cross again, she was grateful now for the moments when they had.

Julie didn't know what the future held, but she knew her past was only a stepping stone on her journey forward. She had changed over that year, but she knew who she was at her core had not faltered. She had often questioned herself these past few months, but one thing had allowed her to rest easy. When she had been called to action, she had risen to the challenge with integrity. To her, there was nothing more important in the world.

At the back of the hall, Julie pushed the door open and walked out into the night.

Did you like *Intrepid Pursuit*?

Hi friends,

Thank you for reading and I hope you had fun!

Did you like *Intrepid Pursuit*?

Please consider rating the book and writing a review wherever you found it online!

If you liked it *a lot*, please consider sharing with your friends and family on social media!

Your support means the world and keeps the story alive.

Thank you again and watch out for smoke the next time you fly!

Your friend,

Billy Hoffman

Made in United States
Troutdale, OR
01/19/2024

17002018R00162